A Joyful  Mother of Children

The Magic and Mayhem of Motherhood

Linda J. Eyre

SHADOW
MOUNTAIN®

Other Books Authored or Coauthored by Linda Eyre

I Didn't Plan to Be a Witch
Lifebalance
Teaching Your Children Joy
Teaching Your Children Responsibility
Teaching Your Children Sensitivity
Teaching Your Children Values
Three Steps to a Strong Family
How to Talk to Your Child about Sex
Children's Stories for Teaching Children Joy

Library of Congress Cataloging-in-Publication Data

Eyre, Linda.
  A joyful mother of children / Linda J. Eyre.
    p. cm.
  Includes index.
  ISBN 1-57345-794-9
    1. Mothers. 2. Mothers—Religious life. 3. Mother and child.
    4. Mothers—Time managment. I. Title.
HQ759.E97 2000
306.874'3—dc21   00-033886

Printed in the United States of America   72082-6684
10   9   8   7   6   5   4   3   2   1

To my high school English teacher, Lewis Munk,
who taught me to write by experience.

To my mother,
who taught me to learn by experience.

To my children,
who gave me experience.

And to my husband, Richard,
who taught me all about experiencing joy.

He maketh the barren woman to keep house, and to be a joyful
mother of children. Praise ye the Lord.
Psalm 113:9

Contents

Section 3

Preface

When the original *A Joyful Mother of Children* was published, I was a struggling young mother myself. I had seven children ages two to twelve. Most days I thought I wouldn't survive. I think the reason the book was well received was that young mothers were desperate for someone who understood their plight. They needed to know that the unpredictable, extreme, and sometimes wrenching experiences they were going through were normal and, in hindsight, pretty funny. It was good to be reminded that the stories of crisis, danger, suspense, intense anger, outrageous comedy, and sublime joy that mothers experience every day with their babies and young children would be impossible for even the most gifted playwright to come up with because those stories come from the minds of the most creative people on earth: children.

I had quickly realized one of the hardest parts of mothering: the beautiful pink or blue bundle they hand you in the hospital doesn't come with an instruction manual. And even though there are lots of wonderful books now that offer advice on what to do about everything from breast-feeding to potty training, there is still very little written that deals with "feeding the mother," or how a mother can train herself to cope with the challenges of parenting. I was challenging myself as I wrote.

The first dozen years of parenting are not only overwhelmingly difficult and sometimes sublimely humorous, they are also the most supremely crucial. The longer I live, the more I realize how vitally important a happy childhood and a joyful mother (at least sometimes) is for the long-term well-being of a child. I had no idea what an impact even the little things I did, both good and bad, would have on our children. Now, with seventeen more years of mothering under my belt, you'd think I'd have everything all figured out. Well, I'm still working on it! Two more children, seven college students, three weddings, three new grandbabies, myriad good-byes and homecomings, as well as a million miles on an airplane later, I have a lot to add. The blissful vacation I had envisioned with only two kids and a college student at home has melted into the realization that no matter how many children you have at home, they are a full-time job. For us, having two at home also means having seven plus children away from home making daily, crucial life decisions. Each needs mail, mentoring, and in most cases, money. What I've discovered is that mothering never ends . . . it just gets bigger and bigger. Yet as *I've* learned from *them* I have grown immensely in what I can describe only as the magic of mothering.

Having passed the half-century mark, I still expect to live as long as my darling neighbor who will turn one hundred in September, which means I'm only halfway through my life. Though I still feel young, I know I'm on a slowly slanting slippery slide to the rest of my life. I expect it to be even more fun than the long climb up the ladder!

My desire is that mothers of young children can read this and feel they are making some progress. I hope that the challenges (and remember to work on them one at a time) I've included at the end of each chapter in section 3 will be particularly helpful. You young mothers need to know that what you are doing is crucial, refining, and heroic. I hope you see that there *is* light at the end of the tunnel as well as thousands of bursts of light and joy along the way. I also hope to dispel the notion that the "Empty Nest Syndrome" is something to fear or dread. I love a soon-to-be-published book about a woman named Ramona Wilcox Cannon, who raised seven beautiful children and then proceeded to publish over four thousand articles after she was sixty years old (Ariel Silver, *Ask Mary Marker: A Guide to the Seasons of Life*).

Both eras of motherhood—those years when the children are all home and those when they are mostly gone (*I don't think they're ever all gone!*)— are exciting as well as challenging. Each has its joys and sorrows. But I must admit that as much as I loved having all the children home, complete with twenty-seven lessons to get kids to, twelve basketball games to watch, about a dozen giant loads of wash every week, and at least nine children to feed three meals a day . . . as much as I loved the precious moments of a family meeting when everyone quit fighting for a few minutes to say what they liked best about the person sitting next to them . . . as much as I loved thinking of nine different prizes for carved pumpkins and helping kids buy eighty-one junky, but thoughtful little gifts to place under the Christmas tree designed just for the kids' gifts to each other (why did I do that?) . . . as much as I loved all that, I'm here to tell you that, for the most part, life gets even better as time goes on!

I am keenly aware that not everyone has nine children. Not everyone has the luxury to travel. Everyone's challenges, though sometimes similar, are different from mine. As our children have started their own families, I am also realizing that the lives of my children will never be just the same as mine either. They will all marry different people and will be blessed with children with different gifts and challenges. Yet, there is something about motherhood that gives all mothers everywhere a common bond. As I have shared experiences about the amazing places we have been blessed to visit and the cultures we have experienced, one truth keeps coming back: The challenges and rewards of motherhood, as well as the need for even greater and more dedicated mothers to keep our families vital at their very roots, are universal.

I have intentionally organized the chapters in reverse chronological order because I want mothers to see the long-range picture before I deal with the challenges of mothers with young children. As our son Talmadge would say, "It's all good!"

Meet the Family

Just to get all the normal questions out of the way before we start: Yes, we do have nine children. They are all our biological children, meaning I went through the "labor" of having every one. There are five sons, four daughters, no twins. Our oldest was sixteen when the last baby was born. They are mostly eighteen months to two years apart in age. I was twenty-three when we had the first one and thirty-nine when we had the last. They possess every personality type imaginable. I didn't plan to have nine children. I planned to have ten. But the Lord makes up for those little discrepancies. We are now lucky enough to have two semi-adopted extras, two incredible sons-in-law, an amazing new daughter-in-law, and the first three of what we hope will become dozens of grandchildren!

Richard, my soul mate and partner, is also my best friend . . . and my best sparring mate. Our marriage has been a success so far because he insists that we "be one" even when I'm mad at him. He taught me how to communicate my feelings so well that he wishes he'd never done it. He is brilliant and funny. He believes in me, even when he's mad at me. Best of all, he encourages me to fly— especially after the dishes are done.

Because there's no way to write about mothering without referring to the children, and because you'll read about our children at several different ages in the book, I thought you might appreciate a brief synopsis of their current status:

Saren graduated with honors from Wellesley College and received her master's degree in education at Harvard. She organizes and directs national conferences to train teachers involved in after-school programs for kids who desperately need enriching education and role models. She is married to her perfect soul mate, Jared, and has just become a new mother. (We are all waiting with bated breath to see what will happen next, as she says she is *never* going to give her child anything sticky!)

Shawni received a degree in social work from Brigham Young University and worked at the Points of Light Foundation in Washington, D.C. She is now madly scrambling to keep up with toddlers Max and Ellie as she becomes a joyful, as well as exhausted and frustrated, mother herself. She and her ingenious partner and husband are enjoying the D.C. area while Richard and I try to figure out how to make every trip include a stopover to see the babies at Shawni and Dave's "bed and breakfast" (bed on the couch cushions and breakfast on the run).

Josh has a degree in construction management and an unofficial degree in computer management. He works in Washington, D.C., as a project manager for Toll Brothers Building Corporation. I can't tell you how many times I've called him crying that I've lost something on the computer and he's miraculously helped me find it. The only thing he loves more than his computer is playing with and caring for children, especially his niece and nephew.

Saydi also graduated from Wellesley College. She is a gifted singer and has recorded her first CD, called "Values Driven." For a year she worked for Family Matters in Washington, D.C., an organization dedicated to orchestrating "Families Helping Families" programs all over the United States. She is pursuing a master's degree in social work at Columbia University. As part of her curriculum she teaches life-skills classes in a special school for high school dropouts smack in the middle of New York City in Chinatown. In her own words, "I am young and single and doing what I love in the center of the world!"

Jonah, was born nine weeks early, escaped being torn apart by two mad dogs at eleven, and narrowly survived being hit by a car going forty miles an hour as he ran across an intersection at sixteen. (We think his life is being preserved for some great cause.) He is a gifted mechanic and writer and is studying anthropology at the University of Massachusetts in Boston, where he and his new wife, Aja, a beautiful and creative junior at Harvard, are living.

Talmadge played basketball for Brigham Young University (he's two or three inches taller than the rest of the boys at 6'9") for a year, and is serving a two-year mission for The Church of Jesus Christ of Latter-day Saints in Campinas, Brazil. He is a perpetual optimist and claims that he didn't mind that he couldn't stand up straight in his little blue house in Brazil because the ceilings were too low. He once wrote, "All my inside activities are either sitting or kneeling activities anyway, so it's perfect. Plus, my landlord has built a little extension on my bed so there's room for my feet." The glass is always "half full" for Talmadge.

Noah played a year of college basketball and then participated in a study abroad program to Jerusalem and the Holy Land. When he served as the student body president of his high school, we realized that the inner magnet he has for collecting friends is there because he honestly can't see their faults. He is a master at remembering "deep thoughts" and can recite one appropriate for any occasion.

Eli and Charity are our only children at home right now. Eli has a great heart and spends most of his time thinking about friends, especially the girl kind. He's a basketball and tennis player and has the ability to be a great student and leader. He has recently developed a sense of humor that keeps us all rolling. With as often as he misses his curfew, he needs to be funny!

Charity, our youngest, came with a gift for copious writing and articulate speaking and an enormous love for children. She is active in her middle school and recently served as school historian. She loses her patience with us quite often; and we can see why, as it is hard to be patient with people who don't know as much as you do. (I'm not kidding. She is pretty smart!)

Our two semi-adopted children were both introduced to us by our children, who met them when they were living overseas. Both sets of wonderful, courageous parents have sent their only children to us to fulfill their dreams of an education and a better life in America.

Eva grew up in Bulgaria and is staying with us while she studies at the University of Utah, majoring in communications. Her grandparents were killed in a concentration camp, and the Communist party ruled her parents' lives until 1990, when communism was overthrown. After a year and a half of full-time service as a missionary for The Church of Jesus Christ of Latter-day Saints in New York City, she has gotten quite a picture of the realities of life, while remaining the most optimistic, effervescent personality imaginable.

Eldar is from the Ukraine. His father is a Muslim and his mother is a saint! Though he sometimes looks as serious as a mobster, he has a dry wit that regularly sends us into unexpected fits of laughter. He is a new convert to Christianity and is studying at Brigham Young University. His dream is to receive an MBA from Harvard and then return to his country to help revitalize and rebuild an economy in shambles.

We are truly blessed with this wonderful family. But before you draw any conclusions about a perfect family, please know that we struggle with life just like everyone else. I told you only the good things about the kids. They consistently lose their coats, are late for school, do silly things with money, break things, get parking tickets, leave their shoes in the hall, and forget to feed the dog. Plus it takes sometimes hundreds of hours to convince Richard that I'm right about almost everything!

In addition, we have had our own dose of real-world problems: Richard's father passed away with colon cancer when Richard was fifteen, after which he helped his mother raise his four younger siblings. Both he and I grew up in families with wonderful parents, lots of love, and basically no money. I have an adopted brother who ran away from home, a half brother who died of alcoholism, and a half sister who died of cancer. I have a niece who, after barely surviving two deadbeat husbands, is struggling to raise her five children on her own. In our own family we have had the usual gamut of problems, including learning disabilities and chronic sibling rivalry, that we've dealt with through a combination of short tempers and longsuffering. Life is real—which is why mothering is so important!

Prologue
Let's Be Realistic: Can *I* Be a Joyful Mother?

This morning I woke up feeling semi-joyful. Actually, Eli, our sixteen-year-old, startled me awake. Bleary-eyed at 1 A.M., after helping thirteen-year-old Charity with a paper the night before, I had inadvertently set my alarm for an hour later than intended. Richard was out of town. The time for our five-minute morning scripture study was past, and I was hurled into the day.

Though I should have been occupied with breakfast as I walked into our newly remodeled bathroom downstairs, I instead became disgruntled by the hard water stains on the new shower doors. Vowing that there was going to be a lesson tonight about hard water and cleaning up after yourself, I began scrubbing a bit to see how difficult it would be to get off the stains. That's when I heard Eli say, "Oh, gross!"

"Oh, gross, what?" I yelled. No answer. "Oh, gross, WHAT?" I yelled even louder. No response. I hurried to the bedroom, where Eli stood looking down at a puddle of dark brown diarrhea on the off-white carpet and, a few feet away, a pale yellow puddle deposited by our darling Labrador, Abel. It was much worse than a similar mess she had left in the family room the night before. I had cleverly closed the door of that room so she couldn't get in. As my teenagers would say, "Duh!" Three thoughts occurred to me simultaneously:

(1) *Gross;* (2) *this dog has a problem;* and (3) *I'm so glad the carpet cleaners didn't come last week!*

I was walking into the laundry room to get paper towels, cleaning rags, and spot remover when I noticed that our cat, Lahina, had slept on my two best, freshly washed tablecloths, which I had left on the hamper until I had time to iron them. (I expected it would be within three months.) As I took a closer look at the tablecloths, I noticed odd brownish-orange, oatmeal-textured cylinders spread across them. It finally dawned on me that for some reason Lahina had thrown up on them, nicely covering the exposed area of both tablecloths.

Back in the bathroom a few seconds later, I couldn't believe what I was seeing. The right side of the new tri-fold mirror on our medicine cabinet had somehow fallen off. The top inch of the mirror had shattered on the tile counter. It had come loose the day before, and I had sent Eli in to tighten the screw. Obviously he had missed something.

Thinking that I'd have to clean up that mess later, I ran back to the kitchen and hurriedly threw a lunch together for Eli as he dashed out the door to pick up a friend. Minutes later, when the brown was out of the carpet just enough to look like someone had dropped a clay pot full of wet dirt on it, Charity came flying down the stairs proclaiming that we were late to pick up a friend and get to school so she could hand in the all-important report she had stayed up working on all night.

It was then that I realized it had snowed about three inches. It was cold, and I didn't think I could even get my car—which is terrible in the snow—out of the driveway, let alone to the junior high and back. Somehow, with only one terrifying slide at the stop sign, I made it.

Back home, I opened the cupboard door under the sink to grab some paper towels to clean up the cat throw-up when I noticed a very distinct, bad smell. *Could I have left a potato under there?* I thought as I pulled out plastic grocery bags, crumpled-up paper, and rusty SOS pads. *Nothing smells worse than a rotten potato . . . except a dead mouse!* I thought, as I saw the very large, very dead mother of a couple of cute little baby mice that Lahina had caught earlier in the week. (At least she's good for *something.*) Suddenly using the spot remover downstairs seemed easy.

The only person home at that point was Eva, our semi-adopted Bulgarian daughter, who was fresh home from eighteen months in New York City. Somehow, giggling hysterically, we decided that her days of living in New York apartments made her the mouse-removal expert. With her nose tucked into her coat to dampen the smell, her mouse-buster gloves, and one of those great multi-purpose plastic grocery bags, she managed to get the mouse in the bag, and I heroically carried it to the outside garbage.

For some unknown reason I must be caught up in a series of plagues, I thought. I tried not to wonder what would happen next. To distract myself, I started to think about writing for a few hours to meet a deadline. The first thing I picked up on the desk was a long-forgotten folder of special papers and letters that I had pulled out the day before while looking for some family history items for Charity's report. My eyes fell on a letter written to us in 1995 from a mother at her wit's end. I couldn't remember ever reading the letter, let alone what we might have written back to help. Let me share a few of this desperate mother's heart-rending thoughts:

Hello, I'm sorry to be taking up your time in reading this letter, but maybe if I complain to you this way, I might not break down. Sometimes I feel so down and depressed and almost useless, it really hurts, but mostly I guess I want to complain to you about money, or the lack thereof. My dear sweet husband tries pretty hard, and I don't think I am a spendthrift, anymore anyway, but there has to be enough and there just isn't.

I know I have made things harder by quitting my job two weeks ago. I just hated my job at the department store. I had put in over six years there, nonstop, talking to customers, placing their large orders with their never-ending supply of money, or so it seemed to me. When it gets to the point that we are now, without even enough to buy our groceries and pay the basic house payments and utilities, I just couldn't stay there anymore.

So now we're worse off than ever. School is close upon us and all the kids will need registration money, lunch money, and of course they want the very latest in clothes, shoes, coats, and backpacks. Not that they will get them just for wanting them.

I know I am down a lot from losing my mother, and now my dad has remarried so soon after. It's very hard. I have lost her and she was my only confidant. She let me cry and complain to her, and she was always so supportive and full of positive statements. It's so embarrassing to tell these things to anyone else. I don't suppose that I will send you this letter either, but somehow, it helps me just to let off steam.

One year ago January, my husband's wages went down by $200, and this was the only cushion we had when we moved. If I had known that this would happen, we would not have taken on this new home. Because of course we expected our wages to increase each year, which has mostly not happened.

All of last year I struggled along when we needed a new washer, then a dryer, and now, a lawn mower and a vacuum cleaner. And the stucco on the house is peeling badly. We never chose to have stucco. The builder just thought it was the stylish thing to do. The deck needs stain, the carpets never have been cleaned. The money all goes for bills and food. I never know where my fifteen-year-old is. The children are always fighting, and I'm so sick of hearing, "Mom, why don't you ever buy us any . . . Band-Aids, tape, salsa, fruit, toilet bowl cleaner, etc." My husband's company has just laid off 120 workers, and he could be next. I'm at my wit's end. I wish John were more supportive of me. He says that I am too negative (I am), and that he is doing the best he can. If only he were not a "white, phlegmatic" personality and could make himself work at a second job. I've learned that wanting it and doing it are not the same things at all.

She continues the letter by explaining all the things she has done to try to make things better, from getting involved with home-based selling companies, one of which was demanding $1,000 by Friday just to get started, to praying and fulfilling church commitments beyond the call of duty to see if heaven would bless her. My heart cried. I could almost feel her pain, and I was so sad about the unhappiness of her life. Suddenly, my terrible, horrible, no-good, very-bad day seemed to pale in comparison to her daily desperation.

I am aware that as joyful as motherhood sometimes is, there are also great tragedies. The difficult realities of not having enough money to buy basic necessities for your children day after day, the agonies of a failing relationship with a husband or a child, the devastating loss of a child, and the horrendous effect of drugs and alcohol ruling families' lives are real. Many mothers' lives are fraught with heavy, unwanted baggage from their childhood. Depression and abuse issues are surfacing everywhere.

Within the past few years one of my wonderful friends has lost two beautiful young children and very nearly her husband in a tragic auto accident. My niece, after surviving two divorces, is raising five children on her own with food stamps, a clunker for a car, and a "power freak" for a boss. A dear friend with six beautiful children is struggling with massive chemical imbalances and a failing relationship with her husband. Another had a wonderful young son who took an overdose of his depression medication one night and never woke up.

These problems make most of us feel a little sheepish about our own. In talking with mothers, they have confided that their salvation has been their faith in God. Contrary to what many naysayers would have us believe, 95 percent of Americans believe in a higher power: A God who loves them and has a plan for their happiness (George Gallup and Michael D. Lindsay, *Surveying the Religious Landscape* [Harrisburg, Penn.: Morehouse, 1999], p. 23).

Although it's no fun to be buried in a trial, those mothers who have passed through them also believe that their trials were great teachers. There may be months or even years when these mothers have struggled to find joy in their lives. Their trials gave them hard times that they never would have asked for. Yet, satisfaction comes from knowing that what they learned in the process is one of their most precious possessions. If we have faith that what we are learning is part of God's plan for us, no matter how hard it seems at the time, we can feel a sort of calmness through our tribulations while trying our best to come up with solutions to our problems. Elisabeth Kubler-Ross has said, "People are like stained-glass windows. They sparkle and shine when the sun is out, but when the darkness sets in, their true beauty is revealed only if there is a light from within."

The answer, I believe, to "Can *I* be joyful despite all my trials and tribulations?" is "Yes!" Not every day or even every season, not in every way or without sometimes wishing life was different, but in your heart of hearts, you *can* know that part of the process of feeling joy is working through your tribulations. If we put the happiness of our lives in God's hands and have faith that we are here to learn from adversity, everything can become a process of feeling joy and its many aspects.

Section 1

What I've Learned

1

Discoveries: Including Ten Ways to Become a Joyful Mother

One of the great advantages of having a lot of children is that you learn so much! Sometimes you learn it fast, and sometimes it takes a long time to learn things that should be pretty obvious. Other things you can learn only with time. Each mother learns different things, according to her own experience. After thirty years of mothering I have learned some pretty useful things. I've learned it's usually okay to be late; things don't have to match; under the rug is a pretty good temporary place for excess dust if you can't find the dustpan; you can wear the same thing day after day and hardly anyone notices; sometimes the best way to deal with an argument is to change the subject; you don't *have* to wash your hair every day; if you wait long enough, some things will fix themselves, even cars; the best thing you can do when your child misses his curfew is go to sleep and talk about it in the morning (Richard would not agree with that one); no one cares if the house is clean but you, but you're the most important; one of the first signs that you're getting old is when you lean over to dry your hair and your face falls up. I could go on and on, but you get the picture.

Looking back, I realize how lucky I have been to be able to stay home with my kids during their growing-up years. There were days when I loved being there right at the moment. Priceless is the only way to describe the days when I could overhear the adorable things my children said as they played house and I could giggle as I caught a glimpse of our renegade two-year-old whizzing down the street to her friend's house in her birthday suit. There were also days when I thought I didn't want to be there. Those were the days when three-year-old Noah put a cassette tape in the toilet and flushed it, flooding not only that bathroom but also filling up the ceiling of the one below. There were days when fishing my new leather shoe (which was being used for a boat) out of the sink was my *best* moment of the day as I leapt from one crisis to another. At the end of those days, I would sigh and moan, "Life is not supposed to be lived like this!" Yet I was there, minus short times when we were away on book tours and for speaking engagements. And I count it as one of my finest blessings. An accomplished actress who had to spend an enormous amount of time away from her children while they were growing up, yet did everything in her power to "be there" for the really important events in their lives, once confided, "I think I was usually there for my children when *they* needed *me*, but I'm not sure I was there when *I* needed *them*!"

Although there were times when I wondered if it was really worth it to cancel a speech or cut a book tour short to be with the kids, I have never regretted it. I have only regretted not fully realizing how short a time kids actually live at home. Sending off our first college freshman made me happy about every day that I had spent with her. Mothers everywhere make incredible sacrifices to be with their children when other things tug at them both single and working mothers feel guilty most of the time. Yet some quantity-time mothers don't have much quality time with their children, just as some quality-time moms don't have much quantity. The multitudes of ways mothers find time to spend with their children is as varied and creative as Martha Stewart's home improvement ideas.

For many years I thought I'd never be walking past the diaper aisle at the grocery store. Before I was married I had a passion for traveling. I dreamed of traveling to other cultures and learning from the lives of people who were very different than I. But this was a passion that I promptly buried after marriage because it seemed to be such an unreachable goal as a young mother. I read recently in my journal that during the first few years of our marriage one of my yearly goals had been to spend one whole day away from the kids! Even though many years *were* spent with the day-to-day routine of raising children, gradually, as the children began to get older, my lifestyle also began to change. As you will find in the chapters that follow, in the end (or should I say in the middle) I was actually able to fulfill my dream to travel beyond my wildest imaginings. For those who want it all—motherhood and the occasional glimpse at glamour and success—I would suggest that you remember that you don't have to have it all at once. Life is long and requires patience!

Another thing that I learn more surely as my children grow and mature is that babies come with very distinct and clear personalities. You don't make them who they are. You just help them refine what they already are. Happily, the absurd notion that children are like clay and can be molded into whatever parents want them to be has changed to the reality that they are seedlings, needing water and light and fertilizer to become who they were *meant* to be. We should no more take credit for our children's abilities to set goals and accomplish them than we should take credit for their gifts of procrastination. They are who they are.

When our second little daughter Shawni was born, it was very clear that she was going to get what she wanted in life. Even though she was sweet and strikingly beautiful, within a few hours after her birth we could see her personality emerge as she let us know in no uncertain terms that she needed to be fed, NOW, and she wasn't about to be putting up with nonsense like bottles and wet diapers.

As she grew, it became apparent that one of the main reasons she had come to this earth was to be a mother. She mothered everything in sight, from the cat to the car. Every child that came into our family was "her" baby. Even as a two-year-old, she followed me all over the house when I brought home a new baby, wailing, "Hold it! Hold it!" as she walked with her little arms outstretched and pleading.

Twenty-five years later, she fulfilled her fondest dream by delivering our first grandchild, Max. One of life's most astounding experiences is watching your child have a child, and then, in the extra light that is present in a delivery room, seeing a personality emerge. Sweet Max was joined by a surprise package—a pizzazzy little firecracker named Ellie—fourteen months later. Their personalities are just as different from each other as their mom's brothers and sisters' are. Some babies sleep all night the day they come home from the hospital (we've never had one) and others don't sleep through the night for three years (we've had two). Some are patient and easy; some are colicky and inconsolable.

With the knowledge that each child comes with his own predisposition, I knew right from the start that mothering was important. What I didn't realize until now, as I embark on grand-motherhood, is that my love and my ability to motivate and inspire and educate my children and help them reach their greatest poten-tial do not stop with them. Although it will manifest itself in different ways, according to the personalities of my children, aspects of my influence (both for good and bad) will last through all the coming generations of time. I have calculated that a mother of three chil-dren, who each have three children, will directly influence about a hundred and twenty lives in four generations of the first hundred or so years of this new millennium.

The best part is that your children take some of the good you give them and make it so much better! After two and a half years as a mother, Shawni's abounding and never-tiring love for her chil-dren, no matter how naughty they are or how tired she is, shines like the unrelenting sun on a hot summer's day. She exceeds my abilities by leaps and bounds and teaches me as she teaches them!

One of my most stark discoveries is that mothering requires training and mental energy. To be effective mothers we must be educated and trained for the job just as much or maybe more than a CEO must be trained to do his job. Because training for what we're about as mothers is so crucial, I formed a new club with my daugh-ters about five years ago. It was called "The Future Mothers of Eyrealm." Richard has his own "Future Fathers" club as well; but I think we have more fun. Once a year, Saren, Shawni, Saydi, Charity, and I, have what is usually a weekend together. We do our business meetings over lunch at a fun place. We try to include an exciting cultural event. But the most important part is that we talk about the value and the challenges of mothering. Sometimes I prepare questionnaires to help us focus on what's important to us individually as mothers. It's a great way to find out what my daughters are really thinking. Sometimes we talk on long car rides about life and what we want out of it. Now that I have two daughters with children of their own and, for the first time, a new daughter-in-law, we have revised the name to "Mothers and Future Mothers of Eyrealm."

One year we did something so exciting that I can hardly believe it happened. I hesitate to mention it, because it isn't something everyone can do. Through circumstances too lengthy to explain, "The Mothers and Future Mothers" flew to Italy—the dream of all our lives—and spent one week driving and sightseeing in an adventure that was beyond our wildest dreams. Together we experienced Rome, with its amazing art galleries and antiquities, as well as the leaning tower of Pisa, the southern coast of France, Renoir's home there, Barcelona, the Loire Valley, and Monet's gardens. We laughed, got lost, had fights, and learned so much about mothering. I think I learned the most!

After one Future Mothers get-together, Saren wrote this poem about her feelings toward the mother, grandmothers, and sisters in her life.

> They create me—
> My sisters, my mother, my grandmothers—
> These women whose hearts are attached to mine
> by so many golden threads of beauty, memories, and emotions.
> Laughter to tears,
> Tears to laughter,

Talking from our minds and from our souls,

Being together in a way that makes words unnecessary,

Praying together, arms linked, or spirits intertwined across so
many miles.

Knowing of the care and the help

that is always so close.

Trials, confusion, fears, needs—

Fading as we look at each others' stories.

Our shared and different passions

magnify each other's possibilities.

Our souls are able to read each other,

in the language of love and pain and hope and reaching

that we all know by heart.

Regardless of your circumstances, talking with daughters about
motherhood (and with sons about fatherhood) is one of the most
valuable things you can do. Making it happen just requires a time
and a place. It doesn't have to be a week or even a whole weekend.
A simple dinner together at a restaurant, with "The Challenges of
Motherhood" as your agenda, can be enormously helpful.
Sometimes you have to negotiate, calculate, and innovate until it
hurts to get daughters free from responsibilities and their own children; but it is so worth the effort. Your daughters are going to rear
your next generation in a wild, weird, and wonderful world. Yes,
they need to do it in their own way, without interference, but they
are also going to need an anchor! One of the most important things
I've learned is that creating a vision of what you want to be is the
beginning of making it happen.

Ten Ways to Become a Joyful Mother

In thinking about what I've learned in the past thirty years, I decided to actually make a list I call "Ten Ways to Become a Joyful Mother." Though the chapters that make up the rest of this section are embellishments of the things I have learned about being a happy mother, I thought it would be nice to create a concise list before we begin. You may want to add your own, but for what they're worth, here they are:

1. *Put first things first.* There are many things that seem important—demands at work, PTSA assignments, clean windows, shopping, and so on—that may be taking huge amounts of time from the relationship you have with your husband and children.

2. *Don't always be logical.* Often logic just doesn't work when planning and dealing with a family. If we had waited for a logical time to have a baby, when there was plenty of money, an extra room, and no outside demands, life wouldn't be nearly as exciting and fulfilling as it is today. If I had waited to run away on a little get-away with Richard or to jump into a new idea when it was logical, I would have missed out on so much fun in life.

3. *Progressively nurture unconditional love.* Unconditional love sounds so easy. But as a dear friend has taught me, keeping that thought foremost in your mind when children don't follow the rules, don't do well in school, become involved in drugs or alcohol, date someone you don't like, or even marry someone you don't approve of, is one of life's greatest challenges. Husbands even have their moments when you find yourself not loving some of the things they do or say. Bemoaning strange habits, bad judgment, and immaturity can obscure the unconditional love that you need to

feel if you don't constantly remind yourself of its importance. Learning not to judge goes hand and hand with this particular "commandment."

4. *Laugh sooner rather than later.* The fewer hours spent in misery because of a daily crisis or disaster, the better. Decide in advance, that when (not if) the next disaster happens, you're going to laugh . . . as soon as possible. The sooner you learn to laugh instead of cry, the happier your life will seem.

5. *Have a formula for dealing with guilt.* One thing that is a given in motherhood is guilt. Especially as children get older and start leaving home, you realize that there are things you could have done better, things you missed along the way, or things you wish you would have done. The best solution for dealing with guilt is to tell your husband or children that you're sorry for mistakes you may have made. Advise them not to make the same mistakes. Remind yourself that there is still time to change. The process of change (sometimes known as repentance) is still a living, working, principle—no matter where we are in the process of mothering.

6. *Put your husband first.* Often as a young mother, although I never said it out loud, I indicated to Richard that he was a big boy and, because a lot of little people were dependent on me, he was going to have to take care of himself. To a degree, of course, this is true, but it is important to remember that having a great relationship with your husband is the most important thing you can give your children.

7. *Educate yourself.* Although it may seem that your own needs always come last, one of the things that can keep your life exciting is to continue to educate yourself, even in the throes of motherhood. To me, nothing is more exciting and stimulating than learning new things. Make time for an art class, a parenting class, a book club, an exercise class, a cooking class. If you find it hard to concentrate on anything but the good of your family, remember that the best thing you can do for them is to educate yourself!

8. *Get help!* If you are drowning (I've learned that almost every mother feels this way most of the time), get help. If you are spending all your time worrying about how to keep your house clean, hire someone else to do it! You may think you have no money for such a luxury and, at certain times, you may be right. But as money becomes a little more accessible, we sometimes think we are a failure if we can't handle our own lives ourselves. Remember that your time is much better spent on the things that really matter. As soon as they're old enough, teach your children to clean and cook. (Warning: This is initially much harder than doing it yourself.) Pay them for it, then everybody's happy. Hire a high school girl to come in and help. Get a cleaning lady. (I've learned that I'd rather have a cleaning lady than a new car any day!) If you're overwhelmed physically, emotionally, or spiritually, think of some ways to GET HELP!

9. *Have a passion for something and remember your dreams.* Think about what *you* love. Contrary to what the children may believe, you are a person too, with a passion for the things that excite you. I met a woman on a plane recently who is the wife of a world-renowned figure. In talking about the ever-present demands of her husband's career, she confided in an unguarded moment of truth, "I've forgotten what it was that I wanted to do." Remember what you have a passion for and, though there are years when that passion will be off in the distance, don't lose sight of it. If you share your dreams with your husband and your children, they'll be much more likely to help you fulfill your dreams, even as you are helping them with theirs. Plus, having passions and fulfilling dreams is a great cure for what is often known as the Empty Nest Syndrome.

10. Have faith. Develop what we call at our house, "confident humility." This is knowing that *without* the help of a loving God in your everyday life as a mother, there is very little that you can do successfully. At the same time, know that *with* his help, there is really nothing that you can't do. It's a great mind-set to have on those days when you feel defeated and it seems impossible to go on.

2

Flying around the World in Eighteen Days Can Be Fun!

I was as excited as a child on her birthday the day that we took off for what I called our "Trip around the World in Eighteen Days." I love to fly! Our assignment was to give speeches—in five worldwide destinations—to members of the Young President's Organization, a group whose membership is made up of young CEOs with companies that net more than 50 million dollars a year. Our topics were "Teaching Your Children Values" and "Lifebalance." Though we had spoken for this very interesting organization in many places, this was our first venture overseas. Our assignments were in Jedda, Saudi Arabia; Karachi, Pakistan; Hong Kong (just months before it was reclaimed by China); Manila, Philippines; and Honolulu, Hawaii; with stops in Greece and Korea. We arranged for two young couples to come to our home, nine days each, to hold down the fort on the home front. Each had a baby of its own. For some reason, having a "visiting baby" was always the main requirement issued by our children when we left them behind. That, and sugarcoated cereal.

When we left, I naively assumed that we would be speaking to expatriates, Americans in the YPO organization working overseas. In actual fact, we spoke to some of the most powerful, wealthy, and influential native business leaders of each country, who for the most part also just happened to be good parents with outstanding families. What we saw and experienced in these faraway places was astounding. Every day I continued to feel like a little kid opening splendid gifts on Christmas morning, except these weren't gifts that would break by afternoon or be forgotten by New Year's Eve. They were remarkable gifts that will last a lifetime.

It is hard to describe the sights, sounds, and smells, to delineate the vast cultures, and to elaborate on the wonderful relationships we developed there in one chapter, so I am going to concentrate on the things that I loved most: what I learned about mothers and families.

A Wedding in Jedda

In Saudi Arabia, what I saw was immensely more vivid than what I had imagined. Upon arrival we were told not to go into the central market square the next morning, as there was to be an execution, and the crowd might get rowdy. I thought they were kidding. They weren't. Immersing ourselves in the world of Islam, which includes more than one billion people worldwide, we were whisked to our hotel. Through the smoked glass of the limousine windows, we were amazed at the enormous number of families we saw walking together up and down a well-lighted esplanade by the sea at 3 A.M., because it was far too hot to walk during the day. Our host's younger sister called our hotel the next morning to invite me to a family wedding. When I enthusiastically accepted and asked her what I should wear, she said, "Oh, anything will be fine! A car will pick you up at 10 P.M. The wedding begins at 10, but it doesn't matter if you are a little late because it will last until about 4 A.M."

Money was not a problem for the YPOers in Jedda. Our host's

grandfather had grown up in a Bedouin tent and had discovered oil on his land. His son, our host's father, had inherited the massive fortune that followed and had seen that several of the mosques in the city had domes that were gold-leafed. Each member of the family, as every faithful Muslim does, gives 3 percent of his gross income to the causes of their religion, a principle that is one of the five pillars of Islam. The other 97 percent of their income seemed to have been spent on every imaginable luxury. All that is a round-about way of explaining that I was picked up for the wedding in the most enormous Mercedes I have ever seen. With a deep breath, I dove into a surreal night that would have made a great movie.

When I arrived at the wedding and saw woman after woman glide across the enormous brick courtyard in her black abaya (a full-length black robe with hood), I realized that I was going to feel pretty naked walking across that same courtyard in my red jacket. It was a long walk, but people knew I was just a dumb American and kindly didn't stare. Inside, however, the cloaks were shed, and I marveled at five hundred women dressed in the most gorgeous Paris and New York fashions imaginable. The colors and fabrics were beyond description. I kept wishing for a fairy godmother to show up with her magic wand and change my dressy business attire into a Cinderella gown fit for the occasion. I quickly realized that the seg-regation between men and women in the Muslim society also applied to weddings. There was not one man there. The groom and the men of the immediate family of the bride and groom were allowed to show up for only about a half an hour for pictures at mid-night. At that time, the most conservative women retrieved their abayas so that the men of the bride and groom's families wouldn't see their faces. Gracious and kind, everyone I met, most of whom spoke English, welcomed me warmly. Once seated, I *loved* feeling like a mouse in a corner, watching an amazing culture go by.

On a stage in front, a large woman in a purple dress with a back-up band sang wild pulsating songs in Arabic. Here and there, women left their linen and crystal-bedecked tables and seemed to love dancing with other women on the stage while the ones who didn't care to dance sat and visited. At midnight the lights went out. Dramatic music played as a spotlight fell on a little boy on a "Gone with the Wind" staircase, who slowly descended the stairs with a gold Koran on a velvet pillow. The bride, in an incredibly sumptuous white dress drenched in pearls, followed him. The diamond necklace around her neck could have been worth a million dollars. Remaining on each step at least thirty seconds, she descended to the floor, where she met her husband and then proceeded to a "Miss America" style ramp. She continued to the stage, where her other family members were waiting. Pictures were taken while the audience watched, and then, to my surprise, they showed a thirty-minute video from old home movies of the bride's and groom's lives. I was informed that a photographer from New York had been hired to do the wedding pictures and edit the video. Amazingly, the video looked very much like what we had seen in so many wedding videos of our own children and their friends. *Children are children, no matter where they live,* I thought as I watched the wedding guests ooh and aah at the cute photos and video footage taken of the newlyweds' childhoods, complete with three-year-old's birthday parties and first days at school.

After the video, the groom and men of the family were excused, and the women removed their abayas, visibly relaxed, and continued to party. All five hundred moved to an enormous room behind the stage, where six tables, each about 200 feet long were laden with what seemed like every conceivable food (although I didn't see any tacos). Ice sculptures dotted the elaborately decorated tables like guardians, and a tent-like stall was set up in the back for those who preferred strictly Arabian food.

By 3:30 A.M. I had absorbed all I could see, hear, taste, smell, and feel for one night. I had had a fascinating conversation with some of the women at one table about their first priority being their families. At a table of older women, I had learned about their charitable work with orphanages and about women who had lost their husbands but weren't allowed to work. Still feeling as though I was walking through a dream, I summoned my driver and tried to slink to the car without too many people thinking, "There goes that weird American woman dressed in red without an abaya."

The Amazing World of the Muslim

Still reeling from the rich experience of the night before, the next morning we continued to soak in the stunning aspects of this totally different culture at our meetings with the Jedda YPO chapter. I learned about the wonderful extended family gatherings that occurred every weekend for most of the families represented in the meeting. Our host explained that his family usually held the gatherings at their summer home just outside the city. When they went far enough away to have to fly, it became more difficult because his father had to send his jet back and forth *twice* to get all seventy family members to their destination.

Their religious dedication was always present. Instead of coffee breaks they took prayer breaks. Without exception, during our meetings they retired to another room with prayer rugs to face Mecca five times daily. The men and women always met separately (I, however, did the men's sessions with Richard. Some of the women felt they couldn't come to the women's meetings if Richard were going to be present, so he abstained). We were amused that their private problems were just the same as members of any affluent society: The men were concerned that the women were too lazy because all their work was being carried out by servants; and the women worried that their children were being spoiled by having too much money. Both sexes agreed, however, that their main concern was the breakdown of the nuclear family.

In Karachi, Pakistan, we were surrounded with a slightly less-stringent version of the Muslim world. Men and women were allowed to interact in public, and the abayas were more colorful and more casual. Masses of humanity crammed into intersections with no lights and no laws. Monkeys perched on owner's shoulders, and the maimed begged for money on every corner. Yet there we met good and faithful families, filled with love for one another, and parents whose biggest concern was keeping their families protected from worldly influences. Children were allowed to come to the meetings; and we saw strong families, loving and loyal, trying to become better. In a dinner conversation with teenagers from two of the families, I learned that teenagers in Pakistan would be amazed to know that in 1997 less than half of American teenagers were having intercourse ("The Naked Truth," *Newsweek*, May 8, 2000, p. 58). Sadly, from what they had gathered from American movies, MTV, other media, and magazines, they believed that monogamous marriages and young adults being virgins until they were married were non-existent in the United States.

One lovely woman took us to see rugs being made by hand in an enormous Persian rug shop. When this mother of four took us to her home to see her own collection of fabulous rugs, she confided that her biggest problem was caring for all of her twenty-three servants. They all had to be fed. And they all had lives full of problems, which she was trying to help with.

When we asked why she needed so many servants, she explained that each child needed a driver and a bodyguard. In addition, their family compound needed guards at every entrance. They also needed servants to cook, as everything had to be prepared from scratch. And by scratch she meant everything from killing, scalding, cleaning, plucking, and cooking the chickens to churning their own butter. Nothing was easy! I vowed to count my blessings the next time I was frantically dashing through the aisles of Costco, throwing in roasted chicken breasts and beautifully prepared cheesecake for a party in three hours.

I thought her guard and protection issues for their children were a little overplayed until we got to Manila. One of the YPOers there also happened to be a good friend from our days at the Harvard Business School in the sixties. As fate goes, our daughters had become best friends while attending Wellesley College together in the nineties. These great parents invited us to their home after one of the regional YPO meetings there. In the car on the way, my friend described the ever-present threat of children of wealthy families being kidnapped. "They are prisoners in their own homes," she said. A child cannot be allowed outside the family compound without supervision. Parents live in constant fear of losing their children. Even the servants are often suspects. The subject had come up because she had asked about our trip to Japan a few years earlier. When I was explaining my surprise at the astronomical price of food there, I happened to mention how strange it was to see a large, orange fish head in a supermarket there that cost $89. She smiled a knowing smile and explained how that particular fish is a prized delicacy of very wealthy families in Asia and the Middle East. There is a procedure that must be followed in eating each part of the fish head. Each portion of the head also must be eaten in a certain order, an order known only to the upper class families. "When children are kidnapped," she explained, "the kidnappers present the child with a fish head similar to the one you saw. If the child knows the correct protocol for eating the fish, the ransom demand is enormous."

A Stunning Lesson in Hong Kong

Again and again I was struck with the realization that despite our differences, there remain amazing similarities between world cultures. In Hong Kong we stayed in a magnificent hotel owned by one of our hosts. It was the only hotel I've ever been in with *real* linen sheets. In a conference room on the top floor the first night we were there, we did a session on "Teaching Children Values." The biggest concern for parents all over the world with a lot of money is teaching their children how to deal with money without spoiling them. Parents want to know how to have family systems that teach kids the value of working hard and earning their own money even while they are very young. This is despite the easier path these parents could take, which is to simply give their children all the money they want.

Parents are also vitally interested in how to teach their children to be honest and to have the courage to stand up for what is right. Teaching them to serve and love others and to be peaceable is also very important to them.

At the end of a very lively discussion that evening about the "how-tos" of teaching children values, a young man named Richard approached us. He was about thirty years old, unmarried, and had no children. He was, at that time, the only YPO member in the world from Communist China. At age three, during the Cultural Revolution, his wealthy, affluent parents were imprisoned and he was taken to a communal nursery. He never saw his parents again. From ages seven to seventeen he was put to work in a factory making envelopes. When he was eighteen he was allowed to take an IQ test administered to every child in Red China. The results put him in the top fifty students, out of millions who had taken it. These fifty were all sent to the finest universities in America, where each one had finished from first to fifth place in his classes. He had excelled at Harvard and returned to China, where he ran a huge business.

When we asked him why he had come on this night, knowing the topic dealt with teaching values to children, of which he had none, he replied: "All my life I have wondered what a family would be like. I have longed to know my parents and feel that I belong. But since that is not possible, I now want to know what a family is, how to organize one, and what to do with one when I get my own. I know that the only way to have true happiness in this life and beyond is through family." The thought of his life without any family ties and his desire to turn that around in his future family took our breath away.

Our flight from Korea to Hawaii, though the most crowded and uncomfortable, was the most fascinating. On board were six American mothers who were on their way home from an orphanage in China. Each carried a gift more precious than gold or platinum. Each had a newly adopted child. Most had waited more than a year for the baby they held in their arms. Some of the babies were obviously sick, abandoned by parents who couldn't cope, and all were girls. Chinese families are allowed only one child. When that child is a girl she is sometimes given up to orphanages or even killed, with the desperate hope that the next child will be a male who can carry on the family name. One mother of a newly adopted orphan said, "This child is not the child that I saw in the picture they sent to me, but I know she was meant for me. I love her and will spend the rest of my life nurturing her."

Mothers Are the Same All over the World

As I finished writing this chapter I remembered the time Richard and I were scheduled to speak at the Polish Embassy in Washington, D.C. Our wonderful friend Irena Kosminska, the wife of the Polish Ambassador to America, had invited us to conduct a seminar on teaching children values for the wives of several other ambassadors and diplomats. This amazing woman is dynamite in a small package. She has a passion for building strong families, especially in her native country and other former Eastern Bloc countries, where under communism, families have been simply struggling to survive, not learning to care for one another. She believes that teaching values is critical in what has been a valueless void. A few months earlier she had invited us to speak at a national conference on families that she had organized in Poland and called "To Love a Child." Her abilities to motivate the media, organize instantaneous translation booths, and orchestrate a call to action were incredible. Now she wanted to encourage other ambassador's wives to do the same.

It was a fascinating afternoon because, as always, we learned more from them than they did from us. After the seminar several of the women who had young children had come to me privately and said that they were glad to know how to teach values more effectively, but could I suggest how they survive as a mother? We smiled at each other, knowing exactly what was meant without going into a lot of detail. Two mothers specifically asked about spirituality, and one wanted to know what God had to do with the way we raised our children. I said unequivocally, "Everything!" I could see by her smile that was the answer she wanted.

That same evening, I went with my daughter Shawni to a book club meeting in the Washington, D.C., area. As we sat and listened to the comments of seven young mothers and heard their concerns about life and love and rearing children as well as their comments about their own survival as mothers, I realized once again that no matter where you go on earth, mothers are the same. They all want to do their best as mothers; they want to rear loving, responsible children and to forge through the refiner's fire of motherhood to become better people.

As I watched these darling young mothers interact, the statement "as American as motherhood and apple pie" flashed through my mind. I thought back through the wonderful mothers I had met on my whirl around the world as well as the mothers at the Embassy, and I knew that motherhood is not just American.

I remembered a shopping trip that Shawni and I had taken to the Pottery Barn outlet a day earlier. Her first concern there was for a nice soft rug where she and her husband could kneel for prayer before retiring each night. I was struck with the thought that symbols of devotion to God are found in homes of faithful mothers all over the world, whether it be a soft rug beside an American bed or a tightly woven prayer rug in a Saudi Arabian kitchen. Whether it is her biological child or an adopted or mentored child, a mother is devoted to children. Whether her roof is gold-leafed or thatched, a mother is devoted to her home. All mothers want their children to be guarded and guided. And well-grounded mothers everywhere want to teach their children to fly!

3

Besides Being Joyful, Life Is Also Funny

Amidst the difficulty of life, seeing the humor in everyday living is often a mother's salvation. One mother wrote, "It was one of the worst days of my life. The washing machine broke down, the telephone kept ringing, my head ached, and the mail carrier brought a bill I had no money to pay. Almost to the breaking point, I lifted my one-year-old into his high chair, leaned my head against the tray, and began to cry. Without a word, my little son took his pacifier out of his mouth and stuck it in mine." Priceless stories like that need to be written down and remembered.

Today, in preparation for writing this chapter, I took a ride down memory lane. Years ago someone gave me the idea to purchase a journal when each of my children was born in which to record my memories of that baby's childhood. With good intentions, I started out thinking I'd write every month about special events that were happening in their lives and the cute things they said. Reality set in and I was lucky to write in them every six months. Then it became a once-a-year recap—but even that was helpful. The original idea had been to give them their books on their wedding day. When some didn't get married by the time they graduated from college, I decided to give them their books then. I was pretty burned out. With Jonah about to get married, I had begun reading back through the story of his life. I was astounded at how much his personality as a two-year-old matched what he has become today! I quickly realized that the stories that were most poignant and made me feel best were the funny ones. They made me laugh. They made me remember how much fun I had had being a young mother!

Kids Do the Funniest Things

A story I had totally forgotten occurred when Jonah was five years old and his favorite thing to do was fly kites. With his $1.69 kite, he and his best friend had been running up and down the street with the wind for about a half an hour. I walked out our front door just in time to see the kite crash into the upper limbs of an enormous forty-foot pine tree across the street. I quietly watched and listened to see what would happen. After trying fruitlessly to dislodge it, both boys gazed up at the red corner of the kite firmly stuck in one of the bushy limbs at the top. Jonah, who was always full of optimistic enthusiasm, said to his cute friend Chad in a very matter-of-fact way, "Well, there's only one thing to do—chop it down!" Amazed, Chad looked back at him and said, "Oh Jonah, you silly boy! You have to *ask* before you chop a tree like *that* down!"

That story got me hooked, and, after recovering from a guilt trip because it had been four years since I had written in any of their books, I proceeded to read through the other kids' books that I hadn't given away.

I read about the day I had come home to Josh, our four-year-old "man of few words," who I'd left with a babysitter and the little sister he loved to tease. When I asked him about his afternoon, I got the usual one-word answers.

"Hi, Joshie," I said. "Have you been taking good care of Saydi?"

"Nope."

"Have you been hitting her?"

"Yup."

End of conversation.

I also came across the funny story of seven-year-old Talmadge, who I'd sent off into the woods to go to the bathroom as we waited for "The Sound of Music" to start in the open-air, hillside theater at the Sundance Summer Theater with about eight hundred other people. It was getting dark. What Talmadge hadn't realized was that just as he "opened fire" in a grove of trees on the mountain side, the spotlight that had fallen on Maria singing "The Hills Are Alive with the Sound of Music" had also fallen on him. He was totally oblivious; but the audience was in hysterics. We sure hoped he couldn't find us until after dark, as he made his way back through the tittering crowd.

Then there was the day I got locked out of our Cambridge apartment on the twenty-second floor, after I had put the first load of groceries and the baby in her infant seat on the kitchen table and gone back for the second load. I ended up finding a neighbor at home three doors down and, in spite of my fear of heights, jumping over balcony railings to get to my own balcony door. Many things had become funnier in hindsight, such as the day my neighbor called to say that she had just watched our three little boys climb out of the upstairs window on to the roof.

Mothers Do Pretty Weird Things Too

Accident prone and clumsy as I am, something pretty funny happens to me almost every day! In fact, just as I was writing this at our tiny little cabin in a snowstorm, huddled around a roaring woodstove, I realized that in my effort to keep my toes warm, the rubber sole of my shoe had melted onto the door of the stove. I managed to extract it, but the bottom of my shoe now looks like a melted ice cream cone, and the glass door of the stove looks like a two-year-old melted a dark brown crayon on it. It's quite artistic actually.

Just yesterday as I was thinking about this chapter, my dear friend Barbara's twenty-two-year-old son Adam had Sunday dinner with us. He told us about the day that his mother had burned the broccoli—for about four hours. It looked so funny that she had saved it. Whenever they moved, which was often, the charred broccoli went with. This past Christmas he had sneaked the broccoli out of the house so he could frame it and write an accompanying poem for her for a Christmas gift. When she discovered it was gone and demanded to know where it might be, her husband told her that he had told the cleaning ladies to throw away anything that didn't look useful, so they had probably thrown it away. Saddened, but resigned, she went on. Needless to say, it was her favorite Christmas present: Her monument to the muddled moments of motherhood.

One of my most embarrassing moments was also pretty funny. It was the day I played the violin with my sister at a funeral. We had played at every wedding and funeral in Bear Lake County when we were children and teenagers because we were the *only* ones in the valley who played the violin. Now she and I were both grown up with new babies and had been asked to play again. Having not played for a while, I was a bit nervous, but we played all the verses of "In the Garden" and sat back down on the front row. As I leaned over to put my violin back in its case, to my horror, I realized that I had forgotten to insert nursing pads into my nursing bra. There were two huge dark rings, about the size of small saucers on the front of my royal blue, polished cotton dress. I know it's not polite to giggle at a funeral. We just couldn't help it!

The Singing Toilet

Whenever we start talking about funny things that have happened to us, my kids *beg* me to tell about the singing toilet. So I guess no chapter about my life being funny would be complete without it. One summer we had the opportunity to take our children to Japan. It was an amazing experience! John and Susan, the wonderful couple who invited us to stay with them for a whole month, had not had a family of their own and wanted to learn what it would be like to have one. I think they got more of an experience than they bargained for. Even though everything else in Japan seemed tiny, their house was enormous by Japanese standards. We had one tatami room (an empty room with straw mats for sleeping) for the girls and one for the boys. Richard and I slept on a thicker mat in an 8- by 10-foot room. Their rent on the house was $12,000 per month. Luckily, John and Susan only had to pay the first $1,000, and his company covered the rest. Things were outrageously expensive in Japan. Carrots, apples, and oranges were at least $1.00 each. Watermelons were about $50. We once saw a 14-inch square box of beautiful cherries, lined up to perfection, that sold for $125.

One of the funny things for an American in Japan is the strange translation of Japanese words into English. They called McDonalds MacDonal'dos. The marketplace was full of T-shirts on which were printed English words that made no sense. They were just a collection of unrelated words printed in English.

One day our wonderful hostess asked if I would like to go with her on her weekly trip to the chiropractor. My back was aching, and she wanted him to have a look at it. I had never been to a chiropractor, but thought it would be an adventure. We took a train and a bus and walked up a long hill to a large house that was the chiropractor's office. The waiting room was a pretty large living room, and the bedrooms off of the main room were the examining rooms. As we arrived I realized that I had drunk a lot of water and was in desperate need of a rest room. While Susan waited I was directed to a tiny room in the corner of the big waiting room, obviously added for patrons after the house was bought for doctoring purposes. It was just big enough for me to fit in. In fact, I had to lean over the toilet to shut the door. As I sat on the toilet, I noticed lots of lights and buttons on a control panel to the right. Below one button was some Japanese and underneath that was an English translation that said, "Singing Toilet." I was dying to know what would happen if I pushed that button, but I calculated that it would be pretty embarrassing if I pushed it and it started wailing out some wild Japanese music through the paper-thin walls, so I stifled the urge.

I zipped and buttoned my pants and washed my hands in a basin about six inches across. As I faced the toilet to flush it, I leaned over to look at the "singing toilet" button one more time. I just couldn't resist the urge to know what the toilet would "sing." As I pushed the button, a stream of water shot out at me with the same pressure as a fire hose and hit me directly in the crotch. I was so startled that it took me a few seconds to register what had even happened. I frantically tried to push other buttons to make it stop; but the steady stream was relentless. I couldn't move to the right or the left to get out of its path, and I knew that if I opened the door, not only would I get the back of my pants drenched as well, but the water would shoot out into the waiting room. I was trying not to scream, as the waiting room was full of demure Japanese folks who were already "bent out of shape." All I could do was wait for the stream (obviously intended to be some sort of fancy bidet) to stop. When it finally petered out, I looked down at myself and saw an enormous amount of water on the front of my pants that could only mean one thing to the people in the waiting room. I couldn't wait. I sat on the toilet and laughed until I cried. I cried and cried. (In fact, every time I tell this story I cry. I'm crying now.)

How could I be that stupid? I thought. Could the translator have meant "squirting" instead of "singing?" (They both start with S.) How am I going to go out into that waiting room looking like this? I was shaking with laughter through my tears. After about five minutes, I got a hold of myself, dried my eyes, and decided to take off my sweatshirt and tie it around my waist with the big part in front. It came almost down to my knees. It looked sort of strange, but not nearly as strange as the water looked on my khaki pants. The doctor, who I couldn't explain my dilemma to because he didn't speak much English, must have thought my outfit very odd as he checked out my back. I hoped he just chalked it up to weird American fashions. That's a day I'll never forget!

Life is always full of surprises. Motherhood would be so dreary and dire if we didn't know how to laugh! Not only is motherhood the second oldest profession, it is also by far the funniest. I love G. K. Chesterton's comment, "The reason the angels can fly is that they have learned how to take themselves lightly."

If you are a young mother, put a blank book where it's easy to find and record the adorable things that your kids say and do that make you laugh. As they grow up, nothing will delight them more than stories about funny things they have said and done. If your kids are grown, remember the wonderful moments that made you laugh, and record them.

4

What Having a Baby and Climbing Mount Kilimanjaro Have in Common

One way to make life a continual soul-fulfilling, mind-expanding, body-challenging experience is to take risks. Motherhood is full of risks. The biggest one is to close your eyes, cross your fingers, pray hard, and decide to bring a child into this very scary world. Sometimes we calculate that decision for years. Sometimes it takes us by surprise. The possibilities of a child being difficult, or having some sort of disability or addiction, are very real in our scary world.

The pregnancy and delivery itself is full of risks. Spending five days with our oldest daughter during her labor, delivery, and post-partum experiences propelled me with breathtaking velocity back into the world that surrounds the birth of a child. An amazing range, in fact an entire microcosm, of emotions fills those hours of labor and delivery: trembling excitement and total exasperation, irreverent irritation and heavenly relief, occasional panic and perfect peace, complete exhaustion and consummate exhilaration, exquisite pain and indescribable joy.

Grinning from ear to ear just outside the door of the very crowded delivery room, where I had retired to listen during the hour of "pushing," I heard Saren's husband, Jared, take it upon himself to be useful and do the count to ten for each pushing contraction.

"One! two! three!" he counted with an authoritarian voice and a little pause between each number. After an hour of animated and dramatic counting, my son-in-law held a precious bundle straight from heaven. With one little purple hand wrapped around each parent's thumb, and grandma's hands cuddling his sweet blue feet, baby Ashton calmly decided that he quite liked this strange new place. With eyes full of wonder, he seemed to feel the spirit of a room so full of light and love that you could cut it with a knife. He was totally unaware of the risk his parents had just taken or of the risky world he was about to experience.

Exploring Risk

There are different degrees of risk. There are the kind that we take purposefully because we want to and because we are exhilarated by the thought of fulfilling a goal. Having a baby, taking a class, organizing an event, taking on new responsibilities at church, at work, or at your child's school, giving more praise, and expressing your love all involve a risk. An even more difficult form of risk involves doing something that you don't want to do just because you know, in the long run, it will be a learning, growing, expanding experience. Saying "no" in order to have more time with your family, starting a new diet, taking a class, opening up an important relationship with a child or spouse that has been worrisome or stagnant, forgiving someone who has wronged you, changing bad habits, and examining and changing your demands on others are all risks that may bring hard times before the growing starts. But hard times are good for us, in spite of their difficulty.

As mothers, every day is filled with risk, but nothing is quite like the joy that comes from overcoming difficulties, from fighting the good fight, and from being delightfully surprised by the joy that comes from overcoming the hurdles.

As our mothering lives go on, it's easy to get in a rut. Sometimes a tedious schedule seems like a way of life with no way out. Our time is consumed with the things we *have* to do. We become almost-robots, filling other people's needs while we stagnate ourselves. One day I realized that it had been a while since I had taken a substantial risk. Adventure is important to me. I had been sucked up in routine for too long.

Taking a Risk of My Own

About that time we had begun talking about the possibilities of going to Africa to do an extended service project. The project involved building a cistern for water storage, making clay bricks for a new room on a schoolhouse, and building desks and helping in a health clinic in a remote village on the east coast of Kenya with an organization called CHOICE. The organizers would not only provide our food, shelter, and materials for the project, they would also arrange for a safari after our week in the village. In addition, those who were interested could stay yet another week and climb Mount Kilimanjaro, which is just over the border from Kenya in Tanzania.

It sounded fabulous to be in a remote village in Africa and actually see all those children I had been eating oatmeal for all my life. (Did everybody's parents cajole their children into eating their oatmeal and cleaning their plates because there were so many children starving in Africa, or was it just mine?) That, in addition to being able to go on a real safari in Africa, where I would be surrounded by wild animals I had only seen in *National Geographic* or in scraggly versions at the zoo, sounded like an incredible dream come true. It was something I had fantasized about doing since I was a child. The prospect of now fulfilling that dream with the added bonus of having some of my children and a good husband experience it with me was beyond my wildest imaginings!

Climbing Mount Kilimanjaro on the other hand sounded like my idea of a nightmare. Totally! The peak is 19,400 feet. We would start at sea level and climb up for five days and down for two. The last day of the ascent, we would need to arise at 11 P.M. and walk all night over a glacier with head flashlights to the summit, where we would arrive at sunrise and where we were assured that the temperature would be below zero. "Who in their right mind would do that?" I raved. *"Because it is there,"* is just absurd! Granted, many people would wonder what person in their right mind would have nine children, but that was something I had a passion for. This is something that I needed like a smack in the eye with a hard rock! I was a non-sports person, extremely klutzy, and terrified of heights.

After weeks of trying to talk five excited children and a semi-excited husband out of it, and after being assured that I didn't *have* to come, they announced that they were going. They assured me that we'd go on lots of mountain climbing hikes in our area to train and get in condition (yippee!), and that I could wait for them at the bottom of the mountain if I changed my mind. The village and the safari would be an adventure, but Kilimanjaro was an enormous risk for me—something totally out of my comfort zone.

Smiling through gritted teeth, I realized that I couldn't bear to be left behind and told them I'd go for it. And even more important, I decided not to whine. I quickly developed a love-hate relationship with the training hikes. I loved the gorgeous vistas and I marveled at the wonders to behold from the ten- to twelve-thousand-foot mountains above the valley where I lived. I couldn't believe that I had spent most of my time outside of home in a smoggy city instead of being thrilled by the fields of bluebells and sunflowers and walking through the clouds I had heretofore only seen from underneath. But I hated most of the going up and was worried about the pain in one knee coming down.

In the end, we packed suitcases full of seven sets of everything, from shorts for the first day of the hike through the rain forest in six inches of mud to seven layers of clothing to keep warm on the day of the final ascent. We packed parkas, snow pants, thermal underwear, neck gear, goggles, and mittens, sock liners, wool socks, Balance Bars, dried fruit, power drink powder, water purifiers, forty-two little bags of trail mix and Gummi Bears (one for each hiker each day), a ton of Jolly Ranchers, as well as water bottles and platypuses in backpacks and a good knee brace.

After months of wondering whether or not I could make it to the top, we arrived at the base of Africa's highest mountain. Two weeks earlier, with fear and trembling, I had seen its snow-drenched peaks (even though it was only a few degrees from the equator) above the clouds on our airplane descent into Mombasa. Literally shaking in my shoes, I watched our porters dump our "stuff" into gunnysacks and swing their loads weighing from fifty to eighty pounds almost effortlessly to their heads. Our first seven-hour day of walking resembled hiking straight up among gorgeous rain forest trees through a mountain of black Elmer's Glue.

To our amazement, and even though we had started our ascent long before they began, those wiry porters, who were about half the size of our 6'6" boys, made us feel pretty sheepish as they swept past us while we struggled to keep our balance with our sturdy mountain shoes and walking sticks. They were juggling their heavy loads on their heads and wearing old beat-up shoes with worn-down heels or tattered sandals. One wore thongs.

Twenty-seven porters carried our gear, the tents, sleeping bags, and food for the ten who were in our group. There were seven Eyres and three young adults who had been with us for the preceding two weeks and who we felt were part of our family. In addition there were four guides who tirelessly accompanied us. They were mostly there to get us through the final assent. The climbing was not technical. There were no crampons or ropes or ice gear. It was mostly a matter of endurance and fighting for air.

Each day held its challenges. Each day we passed through a new ecological stratosphere. After the rain forest came tundra-looking short trees and bushes with white moss clinging to them. The third day's climate resembled a cold desert with only small plants, struggling for air. On the fourth day we lumbered over crumbled molten ash that made us almost feel as if we were walking on the moon. The kids were always about an hour ahead of us, scampering up like little bunnies, while Richard, true to his word, stayed behind with me as did Charles, the head guide. (I think he could see who needed the most help.) I was delighted to realize that Richard was going even slower than I was. The air was getting thinner, and all his training in the gym before we left didn't help much with the lack of oxygen. I had less body weight to manage than he did and was beginning to get a rush of adrenaline, thinking that I might actually make it!

Knowing that the last day would be the killer, Richard kept quizzing Charles as to why we had to get up in the dark and walk to the pinnacle the next day. Charles tried to say that it was spectacular to get there at sunrise and tried again by saying that we needed to get across the glacier before it began to thaw. When he could see that we really weren't buying either one of those explanations, he looked at us with a wry grin and said in his broken Tanzanian English, "Okay, I'll tell you why we get up and walk in the dark: Because if you could see where you were going, you wouldn't go!" Wow, that was comforting! Yet it was also startling to think that most risks are like that. Most risks we might not take if we could see what we would have to go through to reach our goal. Yet, we would never *not* take most risks if we knew the great learning experience and soul enrichment they would bring.

It rained for the final three hours of our walk into the camp on the day before the final ascent. Just as we reached camp it began to snow. It was hard to start the fires for cooking. The flaps on the tents cracked with ice when we opened them. It had been a long, hard day and, worst of all, it was *so cold!* I *hate* being cold! I thought about our lounge chairs at our cabin in the hot Bear Lake sun . . . sitting empty.

We ate what we could. The meat was a bit suspect, having been on the trail for four days with no refrigeration, so we just ate the strange looking vegetables and filled up on the herbal tea and hot chocolate which we had had three times a day in addition to our water in order to stay hydrated.

We were told to go to sleep at 8 P.M., and that we would be awakened at 11:00 for the ascent. Our tent was too small for Richard to stretch out, so he got this great idea that we could stay warmer by zipping our sleeping bags together, putting them over the top of us, and using each other for body heat. I had worn my only coat liner during the day, so it was wet, but I didn't see how I could be warm enough without it, so I assumed it would dry and proceeded to put on all seven layers of clothing for the eminent climb in three hours. The struggle to put on new layers without oxygen just before we left would only waste energy for the climb.

Richard, who can sleep anywhere, anytime, promptly went to sleep and snored. Though I closed my eyes, I was far too cold and worried to entertain sleep. Rather than getting warmer, I was getting colder, and I began to shiver. After two hours, I was shivering so violently that I decided that it was time to wake up Richard so he could give me a little of that famous body heat. As I turned over, I realized that he had pulled the sleeping bag off me in his sleep, which I hadn't noticed because I had had so many layers of clothing on.

The biggest problem was that one of my layers was still definitely wet. Spooning into his warm seven-layered body, I was shaking like an electric vibrator, and he became alarmed. I was alarmed too and wondered how I would ever have the energy to get up and walk five hours to the summit without any air while using all my energy to shiver. I would have given almost anything in this world to be home in my warm pillow-top bed with my down comforter.

In those three long hours, I had my own "labor" as I experienced fear and trepidation, cold and misery. I was second-guessing my decision to come and felt angry and stupid for lying there like a mummy with no sleeping bag in temperatures below freezing. My muscles were already exhausted from shivering.

After what seemed like an eternity, the guides stirred us. I managed to make my joints move me into place on the path, and we were on our way. Once we got moving, the worst was over, but the hard part I had been dreading was yet to come. In a surreal world, we silently followed a long line of about forty tiny twinkling headlamps of the hikers ahead of us. The lights seemed to be hanging in midair as they stood out in the height of the vast blackness of the mountain above us. Even more stunning was what we saw as we looked higher: a black, moonless sky literally shimmering with matted stars, each seeming to be fighting for space.

Victory or Defeat?

One *very* slow step at a time, we progressed up the mountain, stopping to drink directly from our water bladders as our hoses were frozen. I sang "Twinkle, Twinkle Little Star" at least a hundred times in rhythm to my slow steps, which matched my breathing. I sang favorite hymns to myself until I couldn't remember the words anymore because my brain lacked the oxygen to think of them. My head pounded, but I was so grateful to be relatively warm. It was a once-in-a-lifetime sunrise. We were still an hour from the top, but we knew the kids were cheering their success there. As it turned out, they did make it to the top by sunrise, but it was fourteen below zero, and all they wanted was to go back down. Even they admitted that it was the hardest thing they had done in life so far.

We were as happy as we could possibly be without much oxygen when we reached the summit. Our good guides had encouraged us to go slow and find our rhythm, which we did, and we rejoiced in the gorgeous vistas and the feeling that we were at the top of the world! The glacier that we stood on and which surrounded us was beautiful, and we were sucked in by the beauty of the moment. As we stood there, little did we realize that we had just lived through the *easiest* part of the day. The hard part was going down!

But down we went. With my left knee in excruciating pain, even with the brace, but with the help of my wonderful guide, Aman, I somehow managed the three-hour descent to camp, beating Richard by about forty-five minutes. His guide had taken him on a "short-cut." Knowing that he would be dehydrated when he finally got there because we had run out of water hours ago, I went to the food tent for some herbal tea. Crouching down and backing out of the tent, I fell over a huge lava boulder that lay directly in the doorway of the food tent. We laughed hysterically because I was soaked with tea and it looked so funny, plus things are even funnier when you're bone tired. Unfortunately and unbeknownst to me at the moment, I also broke my little finger. We packed up quickly and walked incredulously *another* four hours downhill to our final campsite.

With prescription painkillers not having much effect on the pain in my knee and finger, I decided to turn my attention to my guide who was walking with me. Learning about his life helped get my mind off my troubles. He told me about his three little daughters and wife, about the rough-hewn wood house he had built with his own hands, about his dedication to his church, and about the $6.00 that he gave his wife every week for food. As we encountered mud again, and I told him about washing machines, he became as delighted as a three-year-old at the prospect of Disneyland. "Will you send me one?" he pleaded. I laughed and told him it was a little more complicated than it sounded. He had just told me that his wife had to walk about two kilometers every day for drinking water and that his main job when he was home from the mountain was gathering wood and trying to find enough money to put his children in public schools and feed them. When I asked how they celebrated Christmas, he said that they went to church, had special food, and gave the children a soda.

Poignant Lessons

As we reached the gate at the bottom of the mountain that led back to the real world, with both knees and a finger wailing at me, having slid back down a different, more difficult rain forest trail, I knew that I had paid a lot both financially and physically so that I could take a risk. Yet, the long hours on the trail talking to Richard, watching the kids learn, enjoying the beauty of the earth, and marveling at the strength of body and soul of our porters and guides, not to mention learning about the physical abilities and limitations of my own body, had made this one of the greatest learning experiences of my life. It has taken me a while to realize that despite my miserable night and intense pain, it was worth it. Even now, six months later, with a slightly crooked little finger and the prospect of arthroscopic surgery on my other knee, where I tore my meniscus trying to protect my hurting knee on the last day, I still think it was worth it.

I still believe that taking risks is one of life's great teachers. In risk taking there are always hard times. It's part of the risk package. But win or lose, pass or fail, the learning curve becomes steep, and you learn more in a small amount of time than you may have in years. Of the three amazing weeks that we spent in Africa, the one I personally learned the most from was the one that was by far the hardest and required the greatest personal risk. I learned that I would have been a pretty good frontiersman but also that I wasn't very good at being totally uncomfortable very long. It was a truly soul-fulfilling, mind-expanding, body-challenging experience.

Please remember that you don't have to have a baby or climb Mount Kilimanjaro to learn from taking a risk. I challenge you to inventory the risk factor in your life. Maybe you're in the overwhelming era of mothering when every day is a risk. If so, you're in for a fabulous adventure. Good luck! But if you are not, and your time has become a little more your own, consider taking on some interesting risks to improve your talents, strengthen your stamina, challenge your mental or physical abilities, and help you to boost your self-confidence. If you're going through a hard time, evaluate the risk you've taken and figure out what you're learning. Lessons come, insights abound, and growth occurs whether things turn out as you'd like them to or not. The value of life comes in the adventure, the try, and the risk! First you must say, "Do it!" but even more exciting is being able to say, "I did it!"

P.S. Don't even think about Mount Everest.

5

Teenagers Can Be the Most Fun You'll Ever Have

Oh yes, Richard and I have spent our fair share of time feeling certain that our teenagers were dead in a crevice in a remote place where they would never be found. We've spent excruciating hours discussing every possible excuse a teenager could have for being two hours late for a curfew and at the same time deciding how long it would be before this particular teenager would go out again. It figures that the only time we both went to sleep instead of staying up to wait for one of our late teenagers was the night Jonah and his friends were chased in a car until 2:30 A.M. by gang members who were threatening to beat them up.

As my first child's sixteenth birthday approached, I was excited at the prospect of having some help with car pools and the approximately twenty-two music lessons and sports activities I had to get the kids to each week. Until the first time I drove with her. My exhilaration was quickly replaced with gloom as I realized it would not be a great idea for her to drive other people's kids, not to mention our own. As it turned out, I didn't have to worry. She flunked the road test, as did several of our other children who received their licenses before the law changed and allowed learner's permits to be given out before the driving test.

The most important thing in the world, you see, is getting your driver's license on the day you turn sixteen. I remember one son being absolutely livid and humiliated because, even though he had gotten 94 on the written test, he had flunked the road test. When I asked him what he did wrong, he said through gritted teeth: "Well, I started out on the wrong side of the road, but I got right back over. Then I forgot to stop at the railroad crossing, but it was in a dumb place and it wasn't a real road. If it had been a real road, I would have seen it for sure!"

Since then we've had a few minor fender benders; although I will say it's hard to get a van towed when both tires are popped and both rims are bent on the same side of the vehicle. There have been a few financially devastating speeding tickets and parking tickets. Of course, almost any financial debt is devastating to someone who has only $50 to his name. But mostly when it comes to teenagers, we've just had a lot of fun!

I must admit that we haven't always known what to do with teenagers. We had heard so many nasty things about adolescence that when our oldest teenagers started bringing friends home, we didn't know what to do with them. Richard usually said something embarrassing like, "Where do you guys live?" Meanwhile, I thought that parents were supposed to be seen and then disappear. It *was* hard to have teenagers in our house when we still had little babies who needed naps and elementary-school kids who needed home-work help or wanted to watch Disney movies. But as the years have progressed I've decided that of all the ages, teenagers are the most fun.

Teenagers don't require fancy food. Because our teens' favorite food is cereal, we often have cereal parties instead of pizza parties. I already buy cereal by the giant bag anyway. It's a great, economical food idea when fifteen or twenty teenagers drop by unexpectedly. (I have also learned to keep paper bowls on hand along with the paper plates.)

Teenagers can help you figure out your computer problems while at the same time saying thought-provoking things like, "Have you ever tried swallowing macaroni and cheese whole? It feels so awesome just sliding down your throat!"

At about sixteen, their personalities begin to emerge like balloons that have been cut loose from under the water. Eli, who turned sixteen this year, loves Christmas. It is his favorite holiday. All year he looks forward to decorating the Christmas tree, which the whole family chooses on a family outing when almost everybody is home for the holidays. We hadn't realized how much this little ritual meant to him until last Christmas, when we were in a time crunch on buying the tree. Richard, who tends to be a bit eccentric when not supervised by the children or me, stopped in a rush and picked out the first tree he saw and threw it on the car for a quick ride home. When Eli saw the tree, he was mortified! It was the scraggliest, sickliest looking Charlie Brown tree we had ever seen. For a while Eli ranted and raved, "I can't believe you bought that ugly tree, Dad! What were you thinking?"

Richard said, "Well, let's just put it on a stand and see if it looks any better." No amount of fluffing up, sprucing up, or turning around made any difference. Huffing out of the room, muttering under his breath, Eli soon returned, not with tree decorations, but with a homemade sign that he hooked to one of the bare branches. After about ten minutes, I walked over to the sign to see what was written on the paper. It said, "I was beaten as a child!" Sure enough, that was exactly what the little tree looked like!

Helping Kids Make Decisions in Advance

Contrary to what many parents are led to believe, dating is a fun and exciting time for teenagers and their parents alike. Despite the fact that the world would have you believe that teenagers of the new millennium are a disobedient, disrespectful lot who carry "the pill" or a condom as nonchalantly as we used to carry our purse or wallets, I beg to differ. Even though our teenagers are growing up in a world that is not only a different shade but also a different color, I believe that the silent majority are great moral kids determined to save sex until marriage. In fact, statistics show that about 50 percent of high school kids say they are still virgins at graduation ("The Naked Truth," *Newsweek*, May 8, 2000, p. 59).

Teenagers' lives are made difficult by huge decisions. With that in mind, we have given our teenagers some pretty direct guidelines. First, we ask them not to date one-on-one until they're sixteen. In addition, we ask them to start thinking about their decisions when they are about ten years old. This may sound impossible. For some kids maybe it is, but we must admit that helping kids make some decisions in advance is a secret weapon that helps immeasurably to make the teenage years safer and more enjoyable. So far (crossing our fingers, knees, and toes, with six teenagers down and three to go), we have had some great luck.

At age ten, each child is given a special journal to write in. They bring their journals to a family meeting, where we talk about the difference between decisions we can make now, years in advance, and those we can't make until we get to them. The conversation goes something like this: "Charity, there are different kinds of decisions in life. Some you can make now, and others that can't be made until later. Can you decide right now whom you are going to marry?" (Other options include: Which college are you going to go to? How many children are you going to have? Where are you going to live when you grow up?) We continue with, "There are other decisions that you can make right now, such as if you're going to smoke, drink, do drugs, or have premarital sex. Do you think that if you decided right now that you were never going to smoke that you could stand by that decision?"

We ask our kids to turn to the last page of their journals and write at the top of the page, "Decisions I Have Made in Advance." Then, after we've had a nice discussion with them about possible decisions, we ask them to think about decisions they'd like to make in advance. We ask for their feelings about decisions they will be making about their future good health. They have usually already been taught at school the dangers of smoking, drinking, pre-marital sex, and drugs. Assuring them that we can't make decisions for them, that they have to do it themselves, we ask them to think for the next few weeks about what decisions they'd like to make in advance. We tell them that we're excited to know what they'll write on their list. The kids are usually flattered by the responsibility. We've found that pressure to make any one decision is counterproductive. Only they can decide what they want to put on their lists.

Some kids have had no trouble writing what they've decided to do. Soon they are ready to sign and seal each decision with their signature and the date that it was made. Others take a little longer to think about it. We explain that once they have written down their commitment, there is no turning back. The decision is final. Although we had no idea whether or not this would work when we began, we now have twenty years of experience that leads us to believe that these decisions are one of the most valuable assets to the precarious and sometimes downright terrifying decisions teenagers are expected to make. If they try to make them in the passion of the moment, they will almost inevitably make the wrong decision. On the other hand, if they have thought about it in advance, the chances are much greater that they will respond appropriately.

On subsequent family meetings, we role-play possible scenarios, including the hardest case study we can think of—"you are at a party where everyone is drinking and someone notices that you aren't drinking and offers you a drink. When you refuse, they begin to make fun of you. What will you do?"

Every few months we bring up the subject again, until by the time they are teenagers, they have thought through a wide range of possible dangerous situations and set thoughts in their minds about specific things they are going to say and what they are going to do. Richard has embarrassed kids to their core, asking them about what they think they would do in a situation where they are in a car in a beautiful romantic spot with someone they really like, when suddenly they know they are about to get more physically involved than they should. When asking them what they would do, he doesn't just let them off with a simple answer like, "I'd say, 'I think it's time to go home.'" He makes them say something like, "I would sit straight up, get out the key, put it in the ignition, and say, 'I think it's definitely time to go home!'" Everyone makes mistakes, but the mistakes are kept to a minimum when kids learn how to make decisions in advance. They are empowered when someone taunts them about smoking to be able to say, "I promised myself when I was ten years old that I would never smoke, and I plan to keep that promise!" As the years have passed, and children have begun to get married, one of their prize possessions is the journal with their decision emblazoned on the back page. It is something they will be proud to show their children as they encourage them to do the same.

When our teenagers did start dating, we still went through times of wondering exactly what additional guidelines we should give them in order to help them follow through with the decision that all of them so far have made, to save sex until marriage. After a lot of thought (and dating experience) wise eighteen-year-old Talmadge conjured up three rules that only a teenager would think of. They are so much better than anything we could have come up with that they have now become "family laws for dating." When we had four teenage boys at the same time, they were always reminding each other of these rules. More than one has said that they have saved them a lot of grief. They are: (1) Stay vertical. Absolutely no horizontal positions are allowed. (2) Hands are to be placed only on hands, backs, and heads of the opposite sex. Nowhere else! (3) Three of your collective four feet must be on the ground at all times!

Because I know that these guys are committed to these dating rules, I worry so much less. Teenagers become a lot more fun when you don't have to feel great concern about their values, their decisions, and their morals, but only their safety. Knock on wood.

Teenagers Keep Life Interesting

The incredible new phenomenon of teenagers having to think of creative ways to ask and answer to dances has become sometimes overwhelming, but usually fun and funny. No more can a boy simply call and ask a girl to a school-sponsored dance in our neck of the woods. The more creative the request, the more likely he or she is to go. The more creative the answer, the more fun the date is likely to be.

In a newspaper column recently I read about several bales of hay being delivered to a teenager's home with a note saying, "If you go to homecoming with me, we'll have bales of fun." I believe the story went that the daughter hired a backhoe to carve "I would dig it!" in the "asker's" front lawn. In doing research for this paragraph I was delighted to learn that Noah asked a girl to a prom by burying his name and request in the center of two enormous, well-chewed packs of gum, delivered on a Big Mac bun. She answered by sending a message that she would go with him only if he danced with the cheerleaders at halftime at the next high school football game. He must have wanted to go with her pretty bad.

As I was finishing this chapter, I took a break to go to the grocery store to fill a prescription. Teenagers certainly do keep life interesting. There I met one of our darling neighborhood teenagers, looking pale and absolutely devastated. When I said, "How's it going Jared?" he looked at me with glazed eyes and said, "I'm not too well this afternoon. My friend and I were at the high school parking lot just a few minutes ago, trying to teach one of our best friend's fourteen-year-old friend how to drive. When my friend saw her headed for my car, he screamed, 'hit the brake!' She panicked and hit the gas. I tied the hood down pretty well, but I think we might need a couple of new doors. I'm trying to decide if I should hide the car or tell my parents."

Teenagers might be the most fun you'll ever have!

6

The Trouble with Service

The trouble with service is that no matter how hard you try to give it away, you always get back something more valuable than what you have given. Inevitably, we can never give more than we receive! Every religion advocates service as a way to make life better, but because we are Christians, our motivation for service comes from the words and the example of Jesus. From the time our children were tiny, they loved having a picture of Jesus in their rooms to say good night to. Each child has always had his favorite Jesus picture proudly displayed on a dresser or desk. Each has found a prominent spot amongst the plethora of U2 and Michael Jordan posters to display a picture of their real hero. Whether or not you believe that Jesus Christ was the Savior of the world, as we do, everyone will agree that his teachings of the importance of love and charity for family, friends, and neighbors as well as our brothers and sisters all over the world are valuable and enriching. Not only that, but in speaking of feeding the hungry, clothing the naked, caring for the sick, and taking in and caring for a stranger, Jesus has said, "Inasmuch as ye have done it unto one of the least of these my brethren, ye have done it unto me" (Matthew 25:40).

Because we love Jesus and want to "do what he would do," we committed early as a family to make service an important part of our lives. One of our favorite songs begins with the words, "Because

I have been given much, I too must give." Although we often feel guilty that we don't do more, we're trying. Sometimes our help is just a small thing, like raking leaves for an elderly neighbor or baking a casserole for a new mother. But even those smiles of gratitude make it worth it.

Our best acts of service have been the secret ones. One of our most memorable Christmases was when, through social services, we found a young mother with seven boys under ten whose husband had come home briefly from a job in Texas to deliver the last baby (himself) and had then driven back the next day so he wouldn't lose his job. Our kids tried not to look shocked when we went to their house supposedly to meet them and play for a while, but secretly to see what they needed for Christmas. A better question might have been, "What didn't they need?" There were no windows in their car, not a bed in the house. Our children were awed by their poverty and left full of ideas about what we could do for them for Christmas. We didn't have much money either at the time, but what fun we had giving up a little of our relative abundance to a family who so desperately needed it! On Christmas Eve we left on their doorstep bags and bags of toys, food, and clothing that we had collected from friends and neighbors as well as from our own closets and cupboards. Richard deposited the bags, rang the doorbell, and ran like crazy to join the rest of us in our well-hidden, beat-up, old, gray stretch van, where we were all able to watch the little boys' glee when they found the stash. Our kids were out of their minds with delight and had learned so much about being grateful.

Service projects don't always turn out exactly perfect. When we were living in England one year, we asked our children to give up one of their best toys to a child in an orphanage for handicapped children. Six-year-old Shawni decided to give up her beloved doll, Allison, who came complete with her own bowl and spoon. Shawni simply couldn't believe that when the little girl opened her gift, she was much more delighted with the dish than the doll. Even though the little orphan girl loved the dish more than Allison, Shawni got the much greater satisfaction of knowing she had made someone happy.

One year we challenged our teenagers to find someone at school who needed a friend and invite that person to come to our home on the weekend. Sixteen-year-old Saydi enlisted her friends, who helped her find a young girl who was really struggling socially and academically. First they hung around her locker with her at lunch. Then they started inviting her to their weekend get-togethers. To make a long story short, this darling girl's life turned around. To this day she is a good friend and is proud of the fact that she was able to survive her terrible situation at home and attend the college of her choice. But Saydi felt an even greater satisfaction as she learned the joy of knowing that with love she could help change someone's life.

Africa Was a Service to Us

One of our most startling discoveries about service was made on a recent trip to a village in Africa. This expedition was organized and carried out by The Center for Humanitarian Outreach and Intercultural Exchange (CHOICE). The plan was to help people in a small Kenyan village on the coast of East Africa to build a cistern to catch water from the roof of their schoolhouse. Once built, they could have access to water in their village center without having to carry it on their heads for long distances. In addition we were to help them make large, red clay bricks with a new, manual, one-at-a-time brick press just purchased by the village. Going with us were two nurses, two medical students, and a dentist who would conduct a temporary three-day medical clinic.

As we prepared to leave we found ourselves packing bobbles, bangles, boondoggle, and beads for a village carnival on the last day with them. Thinking that we were going to do them a great service, we packed work gloves, mosquito netting, paper, buttons for sewing onto tattered children's clothing, and soccer balls, tennis balls, basketballs (and a backboard), Frisbees, and board games.

Yes, the adorable village children loved what we brought, and their elders loved having our help to improve their village; but the things that *we* learned in return were astonishing and life changing.

One of our responsibilities in the village was to teach in the schools. We didn't realize until we got there that in the entire village, in schools with about 250 elementary-school kids and 100 high school students, there was not *one* book! We started from ground zero as a few of our more artistic expeditioners made a few books with the construction paper we had brought. The crude little pamphlets showed English words accompanied with pictures. We sang "Head, Shoulders, Knees, and Toes" and the "Hokey-Pokey" (which really did seem hokey after listening to the amazing rhythms the villagers had demonstrated in their welcoming ceremonies). We tried anything we could think of to teach a few new English words to these adorable children, so eager to learn.

Public school is not funded nationally in much of Africa. Parents must pay to send their children even to elementary school.

Only the best, the brightest, and the richest can afford to attend school. Yearly tuition for the high school in the village we visited is about $400, which to an average family who makes about $30 a month is a small fortune. Our new son-in-law Jared, who had just graduated from MIT, had been asked to teach a physics class at the high school during the day. The brightest students begged him to come back to do an extra class that night. About twelve students sat spellbound as he worked through equations with them on the board, with only one small difficulty. There was no light. Watching Jared teaching these rapt students in a cinderblock room with a headlamp on his head and two of us shining flashlights on the equations on the blackboard was magical.

The next day, the headmaster of the high school asked if our CHOICE group would come for a once-in-a-lifetime "intercultural exchange" that afternoon. Our teenagers, along with several of the adult "expeditioners," sat at the front of a large dark room with a dirt floor, facing a sea of black faces. Kids both black and white showed a little apprehension in knowing what questions to ask. There were three questions from the African teenagers that afternoon that I will never forget. They showed how amazingly different the world of these teenagers in Kenya was from the lives of our own teenagers. The first question was from an extremely bright, tall, and handsome boy named Alex, whom we had met the day before. (Even though the villagers were mostly Muslim, each person had an African name *and* a Christian name.)

"What kind of fertilizer do you use?" he asked. The question took us all off guard. Our teenagers hardly even knew what fertilizer *was*. I wondered if 20–40–60 would mean anything to them.

Actually, I realized that it didn't mean anything to me either! Then I remembered that the day before we had been talking to Alex by his small plot of ground about twelve feet square. Growing a crop to feed a family and maybe even to sell was not just a fun pastime; it could mean life or death to these families.

The next question that struck me was, "What animals do you use for transportation?" Our teenagers were awestruck as they thought about the cars in our driveway at home. They had rarely been close to an "animal of transportation," let alone ridden on one! It was amazing to see our kids' minds shift gears and realize what they were being asked.

The third question that just blew me away, especially because it came from a teenager, was, "What do you do for your funerals?" Their questions were so life revealing! I realized that this truly was "a village." When someone in their village dies, everything stops and the whole village mourns for three days. Family members sit by the grave of the deceased for three days, while friends and neighbors bring food and drink to them. The village members prepare special food and they hold ceremonies that are performed only upon the death of a villager. I looked at my kids and realized that most of them had never even been to a funeral. I thought of a recent day when someone in our neighborhood had died (which is fairly often because we live in an older neighborhood) and I had been "too busy" to go to the funeral. Truly we have a lot to learn from these good people.

When the African teens started questioning us, they were totally incredulous when they heard about the Internet and e-mail. Richard did a little game with them and asked them to raise their hands if they had heard of certain names and places. We were amazed (and pleased) that even though a few had heard of Mike Tyson, none had heard of Michael Jordan or Michael Jackson or Madonna. Nor had they heard of McDonald's.

Yes, these high school kids were incredibly grateful for the new soccer balls we had brought. (The little elementary-school kids used rags wrapped up in a tight ball.) The high school soccer team just happened to be on its way to the state soccer tournament and was desperate for a decent ball. But what they gave us was so much more important. By the time our week was over my kids had gone on monkey hunts and cut down trees for the cistern side-by-side with the village kids. They had learned to simply go to sleep at dark (about 7 P.M.) and wake up with the sun (about 6 A.M.) because, without light, there was nothing else to do. A few of the villagers had battery-powered radios and they begged our kids to send them rap tapes when we returned. In so many ways they were kids just like our kids, all wondering about girlfriends and boyfriends, all trying to look their best. Despite the amazing cultural differences, the children, teenagers, and young adults all had similar needs and desires. The knowledge we gained was so much more valuable than any ball, bangle, or bead we might have brought as a "service" to them.

Our biggest regret was that we didn't take books. Though we guessed that their books would be worn and outdated, it had never occurred to us that there simply wouldn't be books in the village. Our favorite village friend, twenty-year-old Saleem, requested when we left that we send him a rap tape and a novel. He dreamed of having his own novel! Jonah, our oldest son on the expedition, had recorded in a journal later that he used to lay awake nights when he was in high school, dreaming of some day having his very own car (a dream that never came true for any of our kids while they were in high school). It was a true wake-up call for Jonah to think of Saleem dreaming of having his own book.

As we proceeded with the week, each little service that we gave came back in triplicate. We watched the compassion on our children's faces as they helped scrape scabies (sores caused by little mites that bury themselves under kids' skin, especially on bare feet and legs) and apply antibiotic ointment and Band-Aids to the legs of more than 200 little children in need. We saw the joy of Africans and Americans, covered with mud, working together to build something for the common good. We saw tired kids doing the back-breaking work of making bricks and carrying rocks. We saw that the rewards of service are unending and what I call one of "the unsearchable riches of Christ" (Ephesians 3:8).

Back to Our World

Recently, most of our children came home for Christmas. I was truly excited about the prospect of a wonderful reunion with all fourteen of us, including our three delightful grandchildren, packed in our not really enormous house. (The reality held its challenges!) I began to plan the agenda. With the kids' friends, skiing, our annual "Family Date Night," basketball games, and the Nutcracker to work in, I realized that a day-by-day schedule was going to be necessary to make things work. I labored over an agenda and promptly e-mailed it to all the children in advance so they could plan their own agendas.

The topic of our Sunday School class the following Sunday

happened to be the joys of giving service. To my horror, I realized that there were no service items listed on our Christmas agenda. Oh, we had done the normal little gifts for the neighbors and had done a couple of traditional service things, but we had not scheduled a family service project. "What's the matter with your mind!" I scolded myself. "Do you think you have to go to Africa to give service?"

I knew that the "Service Queen" and one of the most Christlike people I have ever known was sitting directly behind me. "What service are you doing for Christmas?" I asked after class. She quietly said that she and her extended family were making five hundred sandwiches for a dinner at the Salvation Army the day after Christmas. She gave me the name of a person to call, which I did. The dinner coordinator was reluctant to have "too many helpers" but agreed to let us bring five hundred pieces of fruit if we stayed out of the way of the scheduled helpers.

Even though the family date night and the Nutcracker were fun, our night at the Salvation Army was spectacular! We challenged the teenagers to see how many people they could talk to. Our boys decided to ask the people at the shelter where they were from and what their favorite sports team was. In the process they learned so many amazing stories. Although we had to admit that some faces clearly showed that "nobody was home," most had incredible stories of hard luck and broken dreams.

Saydi found several families who spoke Spanish and was delighted to be back in her element, having just returned from eighteen months in Spain. Shawni was awestruck to find a man from Romania, who she was delighted to speak to in Romanian, a language she had hardly spoken since she had returned from her Church mission there five years earlier.

The highlight of the night came when our darling two-and-a-half-year-old Max, who had just learned to sing "Happy Birthday," found a big, scruffy man with a straw ten-gallon hat on and began singing happy birthday to him as he ate. Even though it wasn't his birthday this homeless man had probably not had "Happy Birthday" sung to him in a very long time. He was obviously moved and delighted as Max began, "Happy Birthday to you. Happy Birthday to you. Happy Birthday dear . . . cowboy. Happy Birthday to you!" That alone was worth five hundred oranges! Giving service is the exact opposite of buying a lottery ticket. (Although I have never bought one.) When you buy a lottery ticket you know there is about a chance in a million that you'll get anything in return. When you give service, the chances are one in a million that you won't have a greater return than your original investment, a return much better than you could have planned or expected!

The story goes that the pride and joy of a certain village in Europe was a beautiful statue of Jesus with his arms outstretched standing in the village square. During the war, the village was bombed, and the statue was severely damaged. After the shooting stopped, the villagers decided to collect money and hire an artist to put the statue back together as best he could. He was able to reconstruct everything except the hands. The hands were shattered beyond repair. Rather than despair, the village council decided to leave the statue without hands and have a bronze plaque engraved at the base that said, "The only hands the Savior has are yours."

7

The Best Secret Weapon Is Praise

In the early part of this century, many babies languished in hospitals and children's institutions and died from unknown causes. In some institutions it was customary to simply give up on these small babies and print the condition of all seriously sick infants as "hopeless" on admission cards.

One of the doctors who was faced with infant mortality on a daily basis was Dr. Fritz Talbot of the Children's Clinic in Dusseldorf, Germany. Amazingly, Dr. Talbot had much success with these sick children. For many years as he made his rounds he was followed from ward to ward by groups of interns seeking new ways of handling children's diseases.

I remember reading about an intern who told this story: "Many times we would come across a child with whom everything had failed. For some reason the child was hopelessly wasting away. When this would happen, Dr. Talbot would take the child's chart and scrawl some indecipherable prescription. In most of the cases, the magic formula took effect and the child began to prosper. Curiosity was aroused and everyone wondered if the famous doctor had developed some new type of wonder drug. One day after rounds one of the young interns returned to the ward and tried to decipher Dr. Talbot's scrawl. He had no luck and turned to the head nurse and asked her what the prescription was.

"'Old Anna,' she said. The she pointed to a grandmotherly woman seated in a large rocker with a baby in her lap. The nurse continued: 'Whenever we have a baby for whom everything we could do has failed, we turn the child over to Old Anna. She has more success than all the doctors and nurses in this institution combined.'"

Although the story doesn't elaborate on the key to Old Anna's success, we know immediately what it was. From the moment we are born, we look for love and unconditional acceptance. The moment those children felt her unconditional love, they began to prosper. So it is with all the relationships in our life.

I am writing this chapter to myself. You can listen in if you want. I often find myself criticizing those who are closest to me. I try to make them be more like me. I try to get them to do things the way I would do them. Sometimes, I even let them know that what they have done is disappointing to me. I nag. I whine. I have even been known to make my husband and children think they are less smart than I when they don't conform with my idea of the way things should be done. Don't get me wrong, constructive criticism is an important key to progress. If my violin teachers had always told me that what I had practiced was just hunky-dory and then had me go on to the next piece, I would certainly have been a music failure. But there is a right and wrong way to criticize.

I once heard a teacher say that a student who had become a successful entrepreneur had taken the time to come back years after her tutelage to thank her and to say: "I don't remember much about what you said, but I remember so clearly how you made me feel! You always praised my efforts. By the time you finished with me, I really thought that there wasn't anything I couldn't accomplish if I put my mind to it!"

Step back for a minute and ask yourself how you are making your husband and children feel. In fact, take yourself even further back to your own childhood. Remember your bed. What it was like when you woke up in the morning? What was the atmosphere of your home from the time you woke up until you went to school? What about from the time you got home from school until you went to bed? Was the atmosphere positive or negative? Now move to your own home. What is the atmosphere there? Similar, or very different?

A couple of years ago, I read a book called *The Color of Water*, by James McBride (New York: Riverhead Books, 1996). It is an incredible story about a valiant, strong-willed Jewish mother who had raised twelve children in dire poverty with two different black Southern Baptist fathers. Each child knew that two things were important to their mother: education and faith in God. The children all had vastly different personalities and possessed an amazing range of challenges for their mother. Each had ups and downs. Each thought a variety of things were important in their lives. But when all was said and done, two things were *very* important to them when they became adults: education and faith in God. The last pages of the book list an incredible number of prestigious colleges and universities attended by this family, as well as each child's way of showing devotion to God. Ah, the power and influence of a mother!

If your children were asked what two things *their* mother believed were most important, what would they say? Although I can't say yet what the second thing would be, I think it would be very nice if my children would think of "praise" as one of the two things that was most important for me to give them, which means I have a lot of work to do!

Praise *is* magic! Last summer we challenged our three children still living at home to earn money for lumber to build school desks in the village we had worked with in Kenya. They did this by painting house numbers on curbs in our neighborhood. Charity called on the phone to make appointments. Noah and Eli, armed with duct tape, spray paint, and stencils, painted the curbs. Near the end, Charity rebelled because the calling was so hard, especially when she got a rejection. So for the last few people on the list, all three of them called and all of them painted. By the time we left for Africa, the kids had earned more than a thousand dollars to build desks in the village school.

One lady, who had been busy when they came by, called later to say she'd like her curb painted and sent a generous $20 dollar donation, twice what the kids were asking. The call came just as we were packing to leave, and we promised to paint her curb as soon as we got back. When we got back, the metal stencils the kids had been using mysteriously disappeared and we were wrapped up in a family reunion. As soon as we got through that, I began to be a nag about the numbers on the Simons's curb. Suddenly the summer was over and Noah went away to college, so I begged Eli to paint the curb. He went to do it, but got waylaid and ended up leaving the new plastic stencils in his friend's car. I nagged again. When he finally went to the house, he spray painted the white square on the curb and realized that one of the numbers he needed from the stencil set must have slipped down in the seat of his friend's car and disappeared forever. I was distraught to say the least! Totally embarrassed, I ran into this good neighbor at the grocery store the following week. She good-naturedly said that she really liked the white square on her curb and was expecting that any day now when she swept the leaves away, there would be numbers there too!

"Eli!" I rasped that night when he got home from school. When are you going to get responsible and paint that curb! I am so embarrassed!"

"Don't worry so much, Mom. I'll do it!" he promised. The first snow came and covered up the curb. I was so thankful that she couldn't see the white square anymore! At the first thaw, I got an idea.

"Eli," I said, when he came home from school. "You are one of the best kids I know. You are being so conscientious about your schoolwork this term. I know how hard you're working, and this semester it's really going to pay off. You are one of the most responsible people I know. You're maturing inside as much as you're growing outside. I am so proud of you!" He was a little surprised, but took my compliment without one sarcastic remark. A few minutes later, after we had gone on to other subjects, I threw this in: "I think Michael's is open today so you could buy a new set of stencils if you have time. The snow has melted, you know. I'd sure love to see those numbers on that white square down on Alton Way when I drive past tomorrow." Nothing else was said. The next day, just before another snowstorm, the numbers were on the curb.

Theoretically, I know that praise is a secret weapon not only to get something done, but also to give kids self-esteem and confidence. It is remembering to apply that principle that's hard. This week, I'm going to try to replace every negative thought with a positive comment. I've tried it before. If I think about it hard enough, sometimes it works. The aura in the house changes from blue to yellow. Children sing under their breath. Dogs lick your hand. (Even though I hate that!) Things get done. It's just a matter of changing habits, which isn't easy.

Sometimes Praise Is a Cultural Process

In some families praise has become a family tradition. It has always been practiced and comes easily and naturally. Other families are quite the opposite. One night after a speech in Hong Kong, where we had talked about kids and money and ways to let kids earn their own money and spend it wisely, one very proper, elegant-looking couple came to us after the meeting and asked if we could have breakfast with them at the hotel where we were staying. The next morning, as we watched them politely eat their breakfast of rice with cream and sugar and green tea, they began to unravel an amazing story about their only son. He was a very bright little boy who had been given every imaginable luxury as he grew up in the world of an only child. The father had inherited the family fortune and had been wise in his management of it. Their son had been constantly surrounded by every lavish indulgence that money could buy.

As the child grew he became more and more difficult to manage and was wildly rebellious by the time he was in high school. The boy and his father had never had a good relationship. They had totally different personalities with totally different agendas. The father desperately wanted his son to take over the family business, and so the parents had decided to send the boy away to an excellent boarding school in the states to begin his training. The boy could hardly speak to his father without engaging in a full-scale argument. They disagreed on almost everything. Over and over again they told us how insecure their son felt in talking with his father because they looked at everything from opposite points of view. The son had very low self-esteem, had done very poorly in school, and was on academic probation. The parents were at their wits' end. Interestingly, even though they knew their son was struggling with his life in general, their biggest problem at the moment was that their son was begging for a new Porsche. He had a nice sports car, but he didn't feel it was good enough. He wanted a Porsche. The question they had for us was, "Should we buy him one?"

Knowing all too well that we were certainly not family therapists (we did highly recommend that they see one on their son's next visit home), several things in their story as they had laid it out for us seemed like obvious places to start on improving their relationship with their son. Our first question to the father was, "Is there anything that your son is better at doing than you are?" The father immediately admitted that his son loved everything about cars. Not only how they looked, but also how they worked. The father seemed totally embarrassed that the son would rather have his head under the hood of a car than anywhere else. We challenged the father, when his son came home for the next school holiday to take him to the garage and ask him questions about what was under the hood of his car, to watch him work, to be amazed, and then to praise him sincerely.

That last statement brought up a wall! There was a long silence. The mother said to the father under her breath, "See, I told you it wouldn't do any harm to praise him!" This had obviously been a point of contention in their relationship. The mother explained that for many generations in her husband's family, praise for a child had been forbidden. It was thought that it would spoil a child and make him proud instead of humble. She didn't indicate whether that was just in her husband's family or whether it was prevalent in the culture. I suspect it was some of both. The thought of praising his son was a new idea to this father, and an uncomfortable one. He wasn't sure he could do it, but he thought it would be interesting to try.

It made me sad to think of this little boy having gone through his childhood without any praise from his father. As our morning with these parents passed, we all began to realize that perhaps what they thought was their greatest asset—their money—was in actuality, their greatest problem. And what they thought was their biggest problem—giving a child praise—might be their greatest asset. We will never know what happened to that family. They were desperate for a change. I would love to have seen it. The more we talked that morning, the more I realized the power of praise in a relationship. There is nothing a child can't do, if his parents think he is capable. There is no finer way to show love, build self-esteem, and foster greatness in a child than to praise his efforts.

Everyone Needs Praise

Luckily I have a mother who was the exact opposite of the father in the preceding story. She was the master of praise! (I have some good genes when I can just muster them up.) Her praise was not just for her children and husband. Everyone in our family, including cousins, aunts, and uncles, thought they were my mother's favorite person in the world because she always praised them so sincerely.

In her later years, she loved providing music for the old people at the rest home. She had her prized possession, her organ, transported to their dining room so that, as she put it, "someone could enjoy hearing her practice." Many were her close friends; and, because by the end she was eighty-nine, most were younger than she was. They always sat a little prouder and smiled a little harder when she came, not only because they loved the music but also because they knew she loved them for maintaining their dignity while somebody fed them. After she finished playing she would always walk around the tables and praise them, even though more than half stared hopelessly into space, giving no sign that they heard or understood. I believe they felt her praise.

In Old Testament times, Isaiah told the people that "the Lord hath anointed me to preach good tidings unto the meek . . . to comfort all that mourn; to appoint unto them that mourn in Zion, to give unto them beauty for ashes, the oil of joy for mourning, *the garment of praise for the spirit of heaviness*" (Isaiah 61:1–3). Like Old Anna, praise holds us in times of "heaviness" and fills us up with self-worth and the will to be better. Wrapping someone in a warm "garment of praise" can change a person's image of himself forever, just as surely as a criticism can crush and destroy.

A friend of ours who is a family therapist says that when he meets with couples who are considering a divorce, they often have a list to share with him. The list contains all the terrible things one has done to the other since their last meeting. "If only they could be watching instead for any little positive things that had happened, I think their relationship would be very different."

This is good advice for me too. I can easily praise everyone around me: the painter, even when he has painted the door the wrong color; my neighbors, even when their kids dump Coke cans on the lawn; my friends, even when they forget to invite me to a lunch; my kids, even when they mess up on a recital piece. But somehow, it is so hard to praise my husband. Oh, he knows I love him, but he's so confident and capable. He already gets a lot of praise. I figure he just doesn't need a lot of praise from me. But I'm wrong. The most important relationships are the ones that need praise most. Praise is a great fertilizer to make good things grow better.

I often think of what Admiral Nelson, the famous British general, said when asked what he would change about his life if he could. After a thoughtful pause, this great military hero said something that surprised everyone: "I would give more praise."

8

Living with the Father of Your Children for Thirty Years Becomes Interesting

A note before I start this chapter: I hope single mothers will be reading this book, as almost half the mothers in the world are now single. If you are one, I suggest that you move to the next chapter. On the other hand, maybe reading this will make you glad you're single! Just know that I know you're there and that you're doing the hardest job on the face of the earth . . . doubled. My heart goes out to you! Single mothers keep asking me to write a book for them. But you can only write what you know. So *you* write it!

An English professor once wrote the words, "a woman without her man is nothing" on the blackboard and directed the students to correctly punctuate them.

Most men wrote: "A woman, without her man, is nothing."

Most women wrote: "A woman: without her, man is nothing."

Funny. Interesting. I think both punctuations are correct in a real marriage partnership if you interpret the word "nothing" to mean "deficient, lacking, not whole." Somewhere at each wedding celebration in our family I like to display this wonderful quote from Shakespeare's *King John*: "He is half part of a blessed man, left to be finished by such as she; and she a fair divided excellence, whose fullness of perfection lies in him" (2.1.437–40).

As I wrote this book, our son Jonah and his wife, Aja, were engaged, and they personified Shakespeare's words to a "T." Our whole family was sucked into the magical realm of "the engagement period." To quote Jonah (with stars in his eyes), "I LOVE love!" To quote Aja (with a dreamy voice and a longing sigh), "I'm getting married in thirty-two days." These two had the most romantic courtship imaginable, including swimming across Walden Pond, traveling hundreds of miles together on wheels—mostly mountain bikes, a tandem bike, and inline skates. They complement each other perfectly; and they laughed and loved as they thought, with great anticipation, about living life together forever. Life was beautiful during this enchanting time. Yet, Richard and I know that everything in their new marriage will not be sunshine and roses every day. Time brings challenges and disagreements, as well as children and differing ways of handling them, which in turn brings brittle reality. Developing a partnership will be Jonah and Aja's most important adventure. It will also be their most challenging adventure.

Someone once penned the lines: "Love at first sight is easy to understand. It's when two people have been looking at each other for years that it becomes a miracle!" Thirty years down the road of our marriage, I can honestly say that I love Richard much more than I did the day we were married. But I must admit that there have been days when I didn't like him very much.

Before we were married, I never dreamed that my husband would eat in bed and then floss his teeth—in bed! I never realized that he would change the TV station at every advertisement and be late for almost every meal. It never occurred to me that he would change his mind every few hours and try to control everything that happened in everyone's lives in our household—forever. Nor did I anticipate that he would be irritated when I organized his jumbled bathroom drawer, and then claim, "Now I can't find anything!"

But I also didn't know that he would continue writing poems for me for every birthday. I had no idea that he would give up a tennis game to take care of me or be ready to drop anything and help one of the kids in distress amidst the pressure of his own deadlines. Yet with it all, I did know that our life together was going to be an adventure!

And adventure it is, albeit sometimes the adventures are trying. On top of that, life gets busy. Husbands and wives often become so occupied that they pass like ships in the night, hardly knowing what the other is doing. At the height of parenting, there is hardly time to talk while trying to put out fires and handle the crises of the day. Our children feel the tension as well. I remember a seven-year-old Noah's answer to four-year-old Eli's question, "Why aren't there as many rainbows as there used to be?" Noah, in his resigned, matter-of-fact way, said, "God just doesn't have much time to make rainbows anymore."

In spite of the hectic nature of life, as the years go by you learn each other's strengths and weaknesses, needs and desires. There is magic in a lasting relationship, such as knowing what the other will say before he says it. Yet, it is so easy to put the needs of your husband second only to the children, the PTA, a clean kitchen floor, the grocery shopping, the wedding invitations, a church responsibility, and the dog's feeding dish. After the children have gone, many mothers realize that not putting a spouse's needs first is a bad habit that is hard to change. No matter where you are in the cycle of life, a husband requires a lot of time and attention!

Our office manager sent home a story one day with Richard that I have chuckled about ever since. As the story goes, a man who was having strange physical health problems visited the doctor with his wife. After a long consultation, the doctor asked to speak to the man's wife in private. There he told her that her husband had a very rare condition, the only cure for which was total tender loving care from his wife. He warned her that it might lead to her dear husband's demise if she didn't get him a good nutritious, hot breakfast each day, pack a delicious lunch for him to take to the office with a wide variety of vitamins and minerals. He added that back massages and, even better, foot rubs would be especially good to alleviate his symptoms. Lots of love, attention, and tender care would be needed to help him overcome his difficulties. On the way home the husband curiously asked his wife what the doctor had said to her. She looked at him with a steady gaze and said, "He said that you were going to die."

We can giggle at that story, knowing that our own husbands' needs are enormous! Still, in our heart of hearts, we know there is nothing more important and exciting than a great relationship with one's spouse. And the kingpin of having that most important relationship is communication. I must admit that my relationship with Richard can be best described as "The Battle of the Titans." The only will that is stronger than Richard's is mine. In our courtship days, when most of our friends were staying out until 2 A.M. for different reasons, we were arguing. To this day, we enjoy a good "heated" discussion. We always seem to get the problem resolved.

We finally decided that we must argue so much because in the back of our minds we know it will be so fun to make up! Once things get worked out, it is hard to remember the next day what we were arguing about. And I'm lucky because Richard insists on "being one," even if it means realizing that sometimes *he* is wrong and is the one who needs to change.

Over the years, we have pinpointed each of our faults. Though we've been able to discover myriads, we both agree that our two worst faults are that I judge too much and Richard demands too much. I make mountains out of molehills, and he makes molehills out of mountains. Just today we came out of our house on a beautiful winter's day with the sun sparkling on the new snow. It was warm, and the snow was melting, leaving just a hint of spring in the air. I loved what I saw, but what I said was, "Look at those rain gutters! They are leaking all around the house and ruining the wood. It's going to cost us a fortune to get that fixed and get the wood replaced." He said, "Don't worry about the rain gutters! I'll fix them! (Something he's been saying for years.) Look at the beauties that you see around you. Isn't it gorgeous today?" I assumed (judged) that he wouldn't get to the rain gutters until the eaves fell in, and he demanded that I forget the molehills and see what was really important.

Another pattern in our relationship is that we are both very sensitive and get our feelings hurt when one says something that makes the other feel less than perfect. (Even though we both know we are eons from being perfect!) In essence, my mentioning the rain gutters told him that he hadn't done what he'd promised so many times, and his words told me that I wasn't looking at what was really important. When we finally figured out these patterns in our relationship, we knew we were on to something big. Now, we are both trying to change. But even if the change hasn't yet taken place, we can at least view the unpleasant interchanges as passing moments of the inevitable.

My biggest breakthrough in improving our relationship came when I decided to work on vexation. Synonyms for vexation are words that often describe my feelings about the illogical, unruly, and sometimes silly things that Richard does. The synonyms include aggravation, annoyance, exasperation, and irritation. When he does or says something that irritates me, I get vexed. And the feeling actually starts at the bottom of my stomach, gathering steam until it spills out my mouth.

When we were first married, it took several years for Richard to teach me to express my anger. I thought the best thing was to just swallow it. But "the gas" that was created from that endeavor built up so much that it came out sooner or later in a pretty ugly form. Over the years Richard has been able to teach me to express my angry feelings so that we can get things out on the table. Unfortunately, he has instructed me so well that I'm sure he wishes he'd never taught me!

Even though it is important to express displeasure, there is a right and a wrong way to do it. Once I recognized that my uninhibited vexation was starting to eat away at our relationship, I started to really work on controlling it. When I feel anger because of something Richard has said or done, instead of blurting out my displeasure, I swallow it like a cow does her cud and think about it for a while. If it's really not worth getting worked up over, I let it go. If it is, I try to find a nicer way to let it out. Once again I have learned that if you want a relationship to change, no one else is going to change until you do. Our life is so much more pleasant when I can follow through with my "vexation commitments." Now, when Richard feels my silence after he has said something a little insensitive and asks, "What are you doing?" I answer, "I'm working on my vexation." He smiles and gets ready—just in case.

A Plan for a Better Partnership

Entire books are written about ways to improve a marriage relationship. I have tried to simplify by writing the four things we have done that have been the anchors of our love and communication with each other. Every marriage relationship is complicated and entirely different from others. Yet there are a few things that seem to work to make a partnership better for any marriage.

1. Be positive, especially when you feel like being negative. Determine to say at least one positive thing about your husband every day. On a busy day, something like "I like your tie" will do. Husbands need admiration more than almost anything. Without it, they tend to wither. Think of something you admire about your husband right now, and tell him about it the next time you see him. You won't believe the amazing things it will do for your relationship!

There is nothing worse than a sick or injured husband. But even when he complains about a sore toe that has kept him awake all night, while you are dealing with the discomforts of being eight-and-a-half months pregnant with a screaming backache, show some positive sympathy.

Appreciation also belongs in this category. One smart young mother realized how often her husband was doing things for her and the children without any thanks. She posted a big sign in the garage that said, "Thanks for always taking out the garbage!" He liked it so much that she said, months later, "It's still there."

2. Create a great partnership. Make time to share goals and dreams. No matter how busy you are, set a time and a place to share your goals and dreams. (We do ours the first Sunday afternoon of each month.) Make plans together so that each of you is not going off on your own track. Don't just think of goals and plans for your outside world, think of ways to create a oneness in your relationship and develop plans to make it come to pass. Probably our greatest asset as a couple is Richard's determination to do everything as partners. There is a fine balance between dependence and independence. It is called interdependence, which is the anchor of a great partnership. We have formalized our partnership by writing it down on paper. Without going into pages of explanations, our plan, simply put, consists of our agreement that Richard is the General Partner for "the outer" portion of our lives, meaning the things that go on outside the household. I am the General Partner for "the inner" part of our lives, or the matters of children and home. We are each "Limited Partners" with total veto power in the other's expertise. In our meetings, he gives me a review of what's going on in the outer world and a review of what's going on in our financial world. I give him a synopsis of family matters as well as a time and place when we can do our "Five-Facet Review," which is the next key to a better relationship.

3. Have a monthly five-facet review. When we were first married, someone gave us the idea to take our parenting stewardship seriously enough to have a monthly formal meeting, with the kids as the agenda. We began by going out to a restaurant with a notebook. We discussed each child and the five facets of each of their lives: physical, social, emotional, intellectual, and spiritual. We would start by asking each other, "How is Saren doing physically?" and go on from there. With nine children, you might imagine that we ordered quite a few courses. We did. But we also found after a few months that what we came out with were only a few things that we could see needed to be done. Richard would commit to read with Talmadge at bedtime three nights a week, and I would commit to make an eye appointment for Noah, who had been complaining about not seeing the blackboard at school. We would decide to have a little party for Saren, who was struggling with friends. The bottom line was not that we were catching problems while they were small, before they got out of hand, but that we were partners.

4. Have fun! Sometimes Richard has a really hard time making me have fun. I can always think of something I need to do that seems more important than a silly, flippant thing he wants to do, such as drop everything and take a hike when there are mounds of laundry to do or go to a movie in the middle of helping with homework. But fun is what keeps life interesting.

In addition to making a relationship more exciting, fun is also a great way to remember that you're in love. Kids also like to see that old people (especially their parents) are still in love and can still have fun. One of their favorite things to do is watch their dad grab me in the kitchen and bend me over backwards for a great big kiss. One of the best places to find joy in a marriage lies in having fun.

5. Make marriage a three-way partnership. Years ago a greatly respected friend and his wife challenged us to always remember that marriage is a three-way partnership, with a loving Father in Heaven as the third partner. When we pray each night before we go to bed, we link arms. One of us begins the prayer and, when finished, squeezes the arms of the other so that he or she can add gratitude and requests. Because we truly believe that God is our partner in creating our family, this keeps us focused and provides a double con-duit for answers and inspiration.

9

Remodeling Is a Lot Like Parenting

It all started one morning when twelve-year-old Charity came roaring up the stairs, screaming that the ceiling was falling in onto the downstairs bathroom. *She's such an actress!* we all thought as she came bursting into the kitchen in a panic. We were busy and promised to go and look at it as soon as everybody was off to school. "I'm not kidding," she insisted. "The ceiling is about to fall on the floor! You've got to come and see it right now!" Dragging both Richard and me by the arm like puppies that didn't want to be put out in the rain, Charity arrived at the bathroom door and we saw that, indeed, the Sheetrock in the ceiling had collapsed, leaving a gaping hole about eighteen inches across. Little drips of water were leaking out the ragged edge of the hole.

Had this been twenty-two years ago, when we bought the house, we would have screamed and panicked and called one of those emergency plumbers who charges an arm and a leg to get there within an hour. As it was, life was too busy that day to sweat the small stuff. Richard had a meeting, I had a dentist appointment and then a lunch, and we just didn't have time to worry about it. Two years before, the upstairs bathtub pipes had rusted through and leaked into the same ceiling that we had already replaced when Noah threw a cassette tape in the toilet and it flooded. After the second ceiling replacement, leaks in the bathroom had become old news. We put one of our old pans under the leak, pulled off the sagging Sheetrock, and thought we'd get to it later.

Three weeks later, the kids were pretty tired of emptying the pan in the downstairs bathroom, so we checked the upstairs bathroom. Sure enough, the entire porcelain tank on the toilet there had cracked some time ago, and the water was slowly oozing out of the crack, through the floor, and into the downstairs bathroom. We were busy with a book tour, so we rubber cemented the crack. We didn't have to change the pan downstairs nearly as often.

In the meantime, one of the sinks in the upstairs bathroom had quit working, and finally the hot water on the only good tap froze as well. Poor Noah was living with a bathroom that had a leaky toilet and only one cold-water faucet that would turn on. But he was busy with basketball practice and games about forty hours a week as well as huge responsibilities as student body president at the high school, so he didn't spend much time there anyway.

On top of this, Richard and I were always fighting over one sink in our tiny master bathroom. It seemed that he always needed to wash his hair in the sink at the same moment I needed to put in my contacts. With our crazy schedule, we had agreed that we needed to organize our bathroom time; but we always forgot.

After a year, we hardly noticed the hole in the ceiling downstairs, but we knew that we weren't going to last much longer upstairs. After my whining became unbearable, Richard insisted that if we were going to remodel, we should be out of the house while they were working so we wouldn't be bothered. It was summer, and we would soon be leaving for a month.

Doing the Deed

I finally rounded up two contractors recommended by friends, and we began the plans and the bidding process. I bought a dozen remodeling magazines and picked out tile and paint for the cabinets. The most important stipulation we gave the nice guy who was to be our contractor while we were gone was that they needed to be finished by the time we returned from Africa, four weeks from the time we left. Just before we left, Richard decided that we needed to put a little extra space in our bedroom where we could put an easy chair and have a little walk-out deck. We also decided that while we were at it, we might as well extend the deck out our bedroom door to make our bathroom big enough to accommodate a second sink. I had spent hours thinking of a great layout for the perfect remodeling job. Richard thought of a better, cheaper one. After bids and consultations, the workers were ready to go to work the minute we walked out the door for our trip.

When we got home a month later, there was a big hole in our bedroom wall and a new, unfinished floor in the master bath. The end. Nothing else was done. The sinks and the tile were on back order, and the painters, plumbers, and the tile guys just couldn't come. They were busy with other, bigger jobs. Little did we know that this was just the beginning of a very long nightmare.

When the tile for one of the bathrooms finally came in, the tile guy built the countertop two inches too short, and the whole thing had to be redone. The workmen had covered over the hole for the light in the shower, and no one knew exactly where it was. One day I left the painter with specific instructions about which paint went where and went to Costco. The color of the bathroom took my breath away when I returned. The painter had painted it dark taupe instead of white. But we liked it, so we left it. If I had a dollar for every day that workers didn't show up when they said they'd come and two dollars for every day they said they wouldn't come and they showed up in the middle of a meeting or a special lunch, I could have earned a lot of money for the project!

One day, about mid-August, I realized that this would be my last chance for years to get the "sixties" bathroom near our front entry updated. Trying to keep cost to a bare minimum, as Richard was going ballistic over the astronomical costs we had accrued so far, I did most of the work. I painted, picked out tile that could be laid over the tile already there, and ran all over town to find just the right medicine cabinet. After squeezing it into my four-door sedan, which required a little more shoving and pushing than I wanted to expose my nice leather seats to, I got it home only to find that it wouldn't fit.

One day the workers took the bright yellow toilet out of the upstairs powder room and put it on the front lawn. For the first few days, Richard read the evening paper there. We thought it was pretty funny, but the novelty wore off after two weeks. Our lawn looked like a wrecking yard with a toilet for a centerpiece. After three weeks of either the tile guy, the plumber, or the grout guy not being able to get there to reinstall the toilet, we considered putting a fountain or planting flowers in the bowl. When we gave people directions to our house, we assured them that after they found the street, we were easy to find. We were the only house on the street with a toilet in the front yard.

Weeks passed. We had decided to paint and wallpaper our

bedroom as long as it was all torn up anyway. One thing led to another. All summer we lived without drawers, without toilets, without sinks. I kept reminding myself that when we had been in Africa, we had lived with an outhouse that was full of bats and had had to carry all our water. This should've been a piece of cake. But, somehow, roughing it in our own home just wasn't as exciting. By this time we were pleading with the contractor to finish by the time school started. It would be getting cold, and we really needed that outside door. He promised to try, but reminded us that he had no control over back-orders, the plumber's daughter's wedding, and the other jobs his guys were committed to. We tried to be nice. But it was getting harder every day!

We attempted to be gone as much as possible so that we wouldn't have to endure the excuses and the dust that was as thick as snow after a blizzard. It filled every nook and cranny, the piano, the plant leaves, even the food. For about two weeks, while our bed was propped up in the living room, we climbed over dressers to get to the double bed in the guest bedroom. It was hard to climb in, and almost impossible to climb out. It was almost like being back on Kilimanjaro!

Before we finished, the stone guy sold the stone that I had painted our cabinets to match to someone else, the floor of our new bedroom addition was stained the wrong color, and the big chair we had bought to put there wouldn't fit. The painter destroyed the out-side door, which had to be back ordered again and eventually repainted. The master bath sinks were lost and had to be re-ordered. The recessed medicine cabinet had to be rebuilt three times, and the bill was three times the bid. On January 8, the contractor came to install the last of the medicine cabinets and to bid us a fond farewell. By then, he was part of the family.

Somehow This Reminds Me of Parenting

Just as everyone assured us we would be, we're glad that we did it—now that it's over. But there are *many* things we would have done differently. Our friends had found a contractor who had put the bid down firmly on paper, along with the exact number of days it would take to complete the job with a clause about the contractor *dropping* the price every day he was late! *Why didn't we think of that!* I wailed, when I told Richard about it. "Linda," he said, looking over his reading glasses at me, "It's over. Forget it. Be glad we survived!" And so we did.

One night when I couldn't make myself quit thinking about all the things we could have done or should have done to make things easier, I thought about what we have been telling parents who are harried by guilt over a child in trouble. "You did the best you could with the information you had at the time," we assure them. "Release yourself from guilt, and go on!" I tried to take my own advice, and it helped.

Besides that, I realized how similar remodeling is to the funny stages our children always go through. So often I have thought. "I know this is just a stage, but I hope I survive it. How many more weeks can we survive this stage?" I thought about the stage when Noah was a year old, and began living in the toilets. There was nothing that he loved more than crawling into the nearest toilet—clothes, leather shoes, and all. He thought it was his own private swimming pool. It was also, unfortunately, a stage when we were trying to get our three- and five-year-olds to flush the toilet on a regular basis. Noah didn't care what else was in the toilet. He just loved the sloshing, sucking sound it made when he moved his bottom up and down in "the hole." It was our own fault for naming him Noah, I guess (except that the water was *inside* the "ark"). For six months it seemed like I did nothing but run around and check to see if the bathroom doors were closed. Yet, at least once a day, he would find one of those doors left open and have a little dip. Prying those little leather shoes off his feet was like trying to get a powerful suction cup off a window. One day when he was about eighteen months old he just gave it up. I don't remember the exact day it happened. (I should have marked it on the calendar.) But he just stopped. Ironically, years later I was telling this story to a friend whose toddler was driving her crazy, and I couldn't remember which child it was. I had to look it up in an old journal. Time is so forgiving!

We all have children who go through crazy stages in their lives. My niece has a three-year-old named Austen who comes to get in bed with them every night. They tried putting him back into his own bed, but often ended up spending the whole night doing so. Finally—beleaguered and totally bushed—they gave up and let him sleep with them. Of course, sleeping with him was like being in a washing machine, so nobody was really sleeping. They quickly realized that he was rolling all around the bed as he slept and often falling out, which is what would wake him enough to go to his parent's bed to sleep. In desperation, after about nine months of this "stage," they thought it might help if they bought him a bigger bed to thrash around on so he wouldn't fall off so easily. It worked—for three nights.

Teenagers also go through stages. At some point in time they inevitably become sure no one likes them and they make your life miserable in the process. Others go through stages when *too many people* like them. We have gone through stages of bullies terrorizing our kids at school, and stages when we hardly saw a child who had enormous leadership and athletic commitments after school. When it comes right down to it, I guess life is just one stage after another. Some are definitely better than others.

The nice part is that even though we think we'll never forget the terrible time we're having, we do. I had to go find old letters to remember some of the nightmare events of our remodeling stage, only two months after the fact. So, wherever you are in your present "stage," hang on! May I suggest the Affirmation Alarm Clock, which I saw advertised in a magazine last night. It wakes you up with positive affirmations, which you can program it to say in your own voice. As you wake to each new day, you could hear yourself say over and over, "I will not let Austen's stage drive me crazy today."

10

The Magic of Moments

I just could not stand the thought of one more Christmas filled with the stress of scrambling for items on Christmas lists and feeling panicked and doomed when I heard, "Only twelve more shopping days 'til Christmas" on my car radio as I madly dashed from Old Navy for clothes requests to the wholesale food store for massive food supplies.

Don't get me wrong. I love Christmas. From the time I was about five years old, my sister, who was a year younger, and I used to start practicing for Christmas right after Thanksgiving. After being sent to bed, we practiced being the first to wake up on Christmas morning and excitedly pretended to wake the other and announce with glee: "It's Christmas morning! Let's go see what Santa has brought!" Sometimes we'd practice for half an hour or more before we dropped off to sleep. Practice sessions included variations of one not being able to wake the other and bumping heads because we both jumped up in the same direction in our scramble to get to the toys. We were snug as two bugs in our double bed, with masking tape from end to end down the middle of the bottom sheet so neither of us could mistake who had the biggest half. By Christmas morning we had exhausted every possible way to wake up and be excited, yet there was nothing like the real thing!

Christmas, though it seemed like a century from one year to the next, was like going to heaven for a day.

Fast-forward with me several decades, a marriage, and nine children later. "This Christmas is going to be different," I would say to myself. "I've paid my dues." I once stood for hours in a long line of frantic mothers at a department store for Shawni's Baby Alive, only to find out that the last doll had been sold to a mother just in front of me. While she and the mother behind me fought over whose daughter needed that last doll more desperately, I tried to think of how to tell Shawni, who had been good as gold all year, that Baby Alive was dead! Then there was the year of "The Nightmare before Christmas," when on Christmas Eve, while setting out toys I discovered that I had accidentally thrown away a little toy robot, the dream of Jonah's heart for Christmas morning. I had hidden it in a black garbage bag in the garage and had mistaken it for . . . garbage.

Richard and I had spent twenty-five years staying up all night on Christmas Eve, putting bikes together for Talmadge, setting up dollhouses for Saren, wrapping Christmas gifts until our fingers bled. Burned out and exhausted, we were ready for something totally different—something wild and wonderful.

A New Idea for Christmas

We presented the following plan to the children still living at home in a Family Council: "This year we'd like to suggest that there be *no* Christmas presents. (You can imagine the faces on that one.) We'd like to use all the money that we would have spent on presents for our family this year for a special project so we can do something for someone else. (The faces brightened a little.) There is a village that is in the high plains of the Andes Mountains in Bolivia with about two hundred Amara Indians who have never had water that comes into their village center or anywhere near their homes. Large jugs of water are carried from springs to their houses by a burro if the family is lucky enough to have a burro; or in old one-gallon plastic recycled oil cans by the mothers and children if they're not. The villagers have spent the last two months digging trenches for water pipes from the wells to their homes and into the village center. They want to be able to see water running through the pipes by December 30, but they can't do it without some help. They need us to help them fulfill their dream of running water. We'll be sleeping in sleeping bags in their one-room schoolhouse in the center of the village. CHOICE will be organizing everything for us and will see that we have plenty of food and clean water. We'll have lots of fun with the villagers as well as doing lots of hard work with picks and shovels as we dig trenches for their water system. There'll be no showers, no indoor toilets, and the food may be a little different, but it'll be good. You'll have a chance to play with kids who've never seen an American, teach them lessons about hygiene, show them where they live on a world map, take Polaroid pictures of people who have never seen a picture of themselves, and play games with little children who will never forget you. We can sign up to go with a group of about twenty people and help them if you want to give up your Christmas presents and festivities this year. We'd have to leave at 6 A.M. on Christmas morning and we won't be back until January 4." To our amazement, the faces were jubilant!

Even though our youngest, who was then twelve, did give a few thoughts to having to face hearing about all the exciting Christmas gifts her friends had received when she got home, she was excited to go. Her stipulation was that we all draw names and be able to exchange one gift on Christmas Eve. The others experienced varying degrees of truly excited and realized they'd just have to find another way to get "the stuff" they felt they needed.

As life goes, the weeks that followed were not the pre-Christmas bliss we had imagined. Visions of reading Christmas stories by the fire and writing thoughtful notes to dear friends since we didn't have to do all that Christmas shopping blurred into the background as we focused on locating ten sleeping bags and mats, searching for flashlights and lanterns, and rounding up kids at various schools to take them to the immunization clinic so we wouldn't have to worry about getting yellow fever and hepatitis A and B.

We spent our time collecting massive supplies and prizes for the carnival we planned to have for the villagers on our last day there. In addition, I started filling bags with "supplementary food" to keep our boys (who need to eat every two hours) happy while they worked, anti-bacterial wet wipes, and first-aid and medications for every possible malady. By the time we pulled out of our driveway at 5:45 A.M. on Christmas morning in two big Suburbans with everybody except our son who was in Brazil and our daughter and son-in-law and their two tiny children who couldn't go, we looked like a veritable circus!

The Trip

I must admit that I worried for much of that twenty-four-hour journey on Christmas Day as we progressed toward our destination. *Will we have to construct our own latrine? Will we be able to sleep with all twenty of us in one room on mats that are pretty much on the other end of the spectrum from our new pillow-top mattress at home? Which of the children will get sick, and how sick will they be? What if Charity whines and Eli complains so much about the food that the cooks who have spent the day preparing it overhear them and think all Americans are spoiled and ungrateful?*

When we stepped off the plane in La Paz, I realized that I had been worrying about the wrong things. The biggest problem was that we couldn't breathe. We were at 13,000 feet, and the village on the Altiplano (high plains), where we would be arriving in less than two hours, was a thousand feet higher. Each breath was labored, and it felt as if someone were loading rocks on our chests like they did in the Salem witch trials.

Along with the other families who had made the trip, we lumbered to the village on a bus loaded to the hilt with huge bags of medical supplies, school supplies, and seeds for the greenhouses. Just as our "wonderings" reached their height two hours later, we turned on to a dirt road and our expedition leader shouted, "There they are. They even have the village band out for us. Be ready to be showered with confetti!"

Sure enough, there they stood at the entrance of a dirt road with a banner and a band consisting of bamboo pan flutes, ukulele-type guitars, and a big drum. All band members were men dressed in simple pants, shirts, and brim hats, except for two old men who were dressed in ethnic scarlet ponchos and Bolivian wool hats pulled down tightly over their ears. The women were drenched in what seemed like a hundred layers of clothing and satin brocade skirts topped by handmade brilliant orange-, red-, and blue-striped shawls. Many women had babies nestled in the folds on their backs. While the band played and it rained homemade confetti, we were introduced to the village leaders with the traditional greeting—a handshake, a half-hug, and another handshake.

Then we had to dance.

Forming a big circle, our lungs complaining bitterly, we all held hands and danced for what seemed like forever. A villager came tearing down the path with a small wooden table on his head, so that we could use it for a party table as they handed out their extravagant treats—small plastic cups filled with Coke and some special crackers—at each stop as we gratefully caught our breath. Then, with smiles at the panting gringos, the villagers urged us to continue the dance, sometimes circling, sometimes dancing, skipping, and dragging, with intermittent stops about every two or three hundred yards. This continued for about a mile (it seemed like five) to the village center. All the while each of us was held by the hand and urged on by a villager. At each stop we asked names. "Como te llamas" (What is your name?), along with "bonita" (beautiful) and "bueno" (good), was about the extent of our Spanish vocabulary. The rest of the time we just smiled and danced, which we came to learn was the ultimate sign of our approval. At one point, I found myself dancing with little Francesca, who was about 4' 6" tall and was definitely the Fred Astaire of the village. Her little feet were going double time, while mine were moving about half of half. Her wonderful, sun-etched, leather, hat-topped face was full of wisdom from eighty-two years of gathering it. It wasn't really hot, but we were burning because we were so close to the sun. Yet it seemed a little absurd to say, "Excuse me while I bathe myself with suntan lotion."

That night, with our skin glowing red in the dark of our school-room accommodation, we settled down to struggling to breathe through the night. We were grateful for the new latrine the villagers had built especially for us, which was so fresh that we almost made footprints in the cement. We were thankful that the villagers, though very shy, had been so kind and excited. But mostly we were worried about the two Christensen daughters, who were violently throwing up about every fifteen minutes from altitude sickness. At last, after every possible dose of medication that their parents and we had collectively brought, they drifted off to sleep. Though every-one did have their day of being sick, that night was the worst because everyone's lungs had to adjust to being without much air.

Although it would take a whole book to explain the joys and difficulties of this amazing adventure, let me just try to put it in a capsule. Each morning the villagers in the fields greeted us as we showed up with our picks and shovels. They would smile shyly and say, "Buenos Dias, Hermano or Hermana" (Good morning, brother or sister). I'm sure they had to try not to giggle while we panted for breath as we dug trenches that were about a foot wide and two feet deep in the dry, rocky soil. They worked circles around us, even though most of them were about half our size. While some of us dug, some played with the kids, some taught in the health clinic, and some taught little geography lessons and hygiene lessons with the help of four or five of our group of gringos who could speak Spanish. Some had a chance to go to the next village, where won-derful volunteer dentists who had come with us pulled teeth. Men, women, and children lined up to have teeth pulled, which without the necessary equipment was the only way to alleviate their pain.

The trenches were dug, the pipes were laid, and the water was coming out of the strategically placed spigots throughout the village on the day we left. During the closing ceremony we realized that these people—who had become our friends without us really being able to talk with them except for a few minutes of legitimate translation—had stolen our hearts. What an incredible experience it was to learn about this amazing culture and the resilience of these good people who lived remarkably rich lives amidst their poverty! The tears popped out and plopped down our cheeks when we saw the gratitude in the eyes of one village woman, who broke tradition and gave us a handshake, a full hug, and another handshake as she bid us farewell. Then, in a moment of inspiration, she took off her shawl and hat and placed it on whoever wanted to have a picture taken with her.

The Moments

I must admit that when we arrived in La Paz at our two-star hotel that night, a bathtub with running water had *never* looked so good! As we lay in bed that night, with the noisy sounds of La Paz as background music, we realized once again that the joy in life doesn't usually come in long stretches for hours at a time, month after month, year after year . . . but in moments.

In fact, I am quite sure that the very best gift of every Christmas season—despite one's age or economic level, notwithstanding the stress and hassles, regardless of the difficulties, no matter where you are or what your circumstances are—is that anyone can experience those unexpected twinkles of joy that make a magical moment. At these moments, you feel true, deep joy because of a great new insight, a beautiful prospect, or a glimpse into the radiance of another soul. They are the magic moments when life seems better than you ever realized, moments when you know positively that the light and love of Jesus Christ is wrapped around you like a warm blanket.

Often as a couple, Richard and I try to share our moments with each other. Years ago we realized that if we were watching for them we could find several magical moments every day, even if it wasn't Christmas. At the end of a hard day, we love saying, "Do you want to hear my moment?" In that noisy little hotel room, we tried to re-congregate moments from our wonderful Christmas adventure in our minds. There were so many.

During "The Dance" on the night before our departure, when these dear villagers had persuaded a band to come all the way from a university in La Paz to entertain us with folk music, we, of course, ended up dancing with them. They had even rigged up a light out in the village square, where we had played in the dark with the village kids on the other nights. I was happy to have the excuse to take pictures for the first part of the evening so I could watch for the moments. I was also happy not to be among those on our expedition gasping for breath as they jumped and twirled, lungs bursting with pain, until the end of each fifteen-minute song. I noticed the pure pleasure on the face of the leader of the village band as he tipped his head from side to side and clapped his hands to the music with a contented smile. As I enjoyed watching all our children holding hands in a circle dance, I noticed that Charity was wearing a red sweater exactly the same color as the sweater of the little Bolivian girl straight across the circle. As they hopped and skipped to the music, they both turned to my camera at the exact same instant with a look on their faces that said, "This is the happiest night of my life!"

Richard remembered one afternoon when we had been digging trenches for several hours and having family contests to see who could dig fastest. We were near Eduardo's house, who had been elected a village councilman. Three of his little children somehow got involved in a chasing game with Noah. He dropped his pick and began chasing them and swinging them around in the air when he caught one. They, of course, squealed with delight and soon learned that this giant (6'6") couldn't really catch them unless they ran really slow. The sheer delight on their faces created a picture in our minds that we'll never forget.

Saydi, who was the only one of us who could speak fluent Spanish, provided many wonderful moments. She was in her glory! We glowed in the moment as we watched her teach a small group of village health care workers about human reproduction. As her audience giggled politely, our expedition leader and nurse Evelyn told us that she had started out by saying, "I think that my face is going to be red while I give you this lesson, but the things I am going to tell you are very important!" Watching Saydi teach personal hygiene by reading the village children a story called "Pigpen Mary" was also a delight as we observed her rapt audience watching her with awe. These are the same kids that the day before had been filled with light as she taught them to sing, in Spanish, a song about being a child of God. They were also the ones who had crowded around her when she showed them where on earth they lived on the blow-up world globe we had brought. Saydi was the only one who begged, "Leave me here!" on our last day in the village.

What a moment it was to see our oldest daughter, Saren (who had been single for twenty-eight years and had married shortly before we left), walking off to the hills with a shovel in one hand and new husband Jared's hand in the other as she obviously relished experiencing this first great adventure with him! Jared, a farm boy from Idaho, who worked circles around the rest of us and was in his last year at MIT, was the engineer these villagers needed to figure out how to connect the pipe coming from the large cement cistern that collected the spring water to the pipes that lay in the trenches. He was there to see the moment of pure joy and disbelief on the faces of the villagers (many of whom had had doubts about whether or not the system would really work) when the fresh water actually ran through the pipes and came out the first spigot.

Great moments simply flooded our minds as we remembered the determination on Josh's face as he worked on mounting and erecting the basketball backboard and hoop we had brought, and the excitement in his face as he showed the villagers how to play. We remembered fifteen-year-old Eli's excitement at setting up the speakers we had bought at the duty-free shop in Miami to a little CD player one night because the native teenagers had asked to hear American music. His face was beaming as they huddled around a slab of cement in the dark with wool hats and coats on a night cold enough to send into the air puffs of steam from each nose and mouth. Some of our kids demonstrated "swing dancing," a novel idea to these shy and curious young Bolivians.

One final moment happened after we had all loaded onto the bus and the band had played their farewell. Although the villagers were begging us to stay and dance, we needed to get to the site of some ancient ruins before the gates were closed. With the bus motor running, the native "Director of the Water Project" with the village's biggest grin, who Jonah had named Tony because he couldn't pronounce his real name, came running toward the bus. Twenty-one-year old Jonah had worked with him elbow-to-elbow and laughed and joked with him all week, and they had become best friends. Tony jumped on the bus as it was pulling out and yelled, "Honas, Honas, Where is Honas?" followed by indiscernible Spanish pleas. Translators quickly revealed that he was saying, "Jonah, come on, one more dance, just one more dance!" Jonah peeled out of that bus, and we all basked in the moment of seeing these great friends have one last funny, jumpy dance together before they would never see each other again.

Yes, these are poignant moments from a very grand adventure, but as we re-entered life as we know it, we knew that it wasn't just this Christmas or this adventure that contained those magical moments. Though life is inevitably filled with stress, these moments of joy, which are tiny bursts of feeling the pure love of Christ and the light of the Savior, are truly the greatest gifts of the Christmas season. Each one of those crazy, hassle-ridden Christmases between the ones as a child and the ones now as parents and grandparents are dripping with wonderful moments. Not only that, those moments continue throughout the year. The problem is that we often miss them because we get so caught up in survival that we aren't watching for them. Scouting for "moments" as we progress through a grizzly day and remembering them with a smile is what joy is all about.

In the end, the joy of those moments in the high plains of Bolivia felt almost exactly the same as the joy I felt on the first Christmas I can remember after my sister and I had spent all those hours "practicing waking up." As I rocked in my new little rocking chair with the doll of my dreams—Roberta—in my lap by what seemed like the most beautiful Christmas tree in the world with its bubble lights, colored balls, and shimmering silver icicles, amongst a sea of wrapping paper and such extravagant gifts as a bottle of fake perfume and new roller skates, I knew that life was beautiful.

Especially for Mothers of Young Children

11

Especially for Mothers of Young Children

Having children, whether it is by natural causes, by adoption, by semi-adopting, or by seeing a child with a need and filling it, is the most noble process on earth. Last week in the grocery store a mother stopped me with a beautiful tiny, pink bundle in an infant seat. "You don't know me," she said, "but I know you, and I just have to ask you a question." Wishing I had brushed my hair and feeling a little squirmy because I had to get kids to the airport in a couple of hours, I soon forgot it all as she sucked me into an amazing story.

"This baby was adopted five months ago," she said. "She is the younger sibling of our ten-year-old daughter, who was also adopted. We also have an eight-year-old who was adopted. He is our most difficult child, but is brilliant and has an amazing singing voice straight from heaven. Last week his mother called me begging me to adopt her three-and-a-half-year-old twins. I had offered to take them when they were eighteen months old, but she couldn't bear to give them up. Now, her alcoholism has gotten the best of her and she realized that they would be much better off with us."

As we went through the wide variety of possible angles of this major adoption decision, I realized that she and her husband were not taking this decision lightly. They had thought through every possible scenario, including the effect of the adoption on each of their other children, one of whom was an adopted five-year-old and would be the only child not to have a biological sibling in the family. She was also rightly worried about the long-term effects of an unhappy childhood on the twins. As we talked, I realized that this amazing mother was not asking me to advise her about whether or not to go through with the adoption. Her decision seemed to be made. She wanted to know if I knew a good child psychiatrist for one of the twins, who was already showing signs of anger and rebellion. What a woman! Magnificent as she was, I knew, as she did, that there would be a lot of tough times ahead! It also reminded me again that each mother of young children has her own challenges. Each of us is different and yet, in so many ways, we all struggle with the same dilemmas. The hard part is to remain happy and positive amidst what sometimes seems incredible adversity.

When I wrote the original *A Joyful Mother of Children* in 1983, that phrase from Psalm 113:9 seemed as refreshing as a cool breeze blowing through a hot Thanksgiving Day kitchen. I loved the concept of being "a joyful mother," mostly because, even though in my heart of hearts I was happy, I kept forgetting to feel joy. In my day-to-day attempts to survive seven children under twelve and a wonderful but hyperactive husband, I felt that one of my greatest needs was to be more joyful. From talking to other mothers in the midst of the muddle of managing motherhood at what seemed like its height and breadth, I realized that they too wanted to feel more joy.

In thinking about being a joyful mother, I have re-read and studied Psalm 113:9 and remembered that I didn't include the whole verse in the original book because I didn't really like it very

much. Somehow it didn't sound very fun. It talked about house-
keeping and being barren. As far as I knew, being barren meant
being unfertile and unable to have children; and my feelings about
keeping house have never been very positive. Plus, I didn't have
time to look into it. Somebody had probably kicked a hole in the
wall or the baby had fallen down the stairs just as I was about to
study what that verse actually meant, so I simply went with the part
that made me feel good.

The whole verse reads like this: "He maketh the barren woman
to keep house, and to be a joyful mother of children. Praise ye the
Lord."

In perspective, I've decided that it *does* give one joy to keep
house. I don't really like the dusting and ironing part very much,
although a long day of uninterrupted cleaning, which happens only
on rare occasions, does give you time to think while you work and a
sense of accomplishment when you're finished, even if you'd rather
be doing something else. But I think "to keep house" means more
than working with Windex and Pledge. To me it means building an
atmosphere at home where husband and kids want to be, where
they like bringing their friends, where memories are made, and
where they can be inspired to fulfill their dreams.

Next, the word "barren" needs to be worked out. To my surprise,
I looked it up in the dictionary and found an enormous list of
synonyms, only two of which were "unfertile and childless." In fact,
I realized that I could write a whole chapter about how each
synonym of the word barren had described *me* on different days of
my life. If any of these synonyms also sounds familiar to you, I guess
you'd better read on. *Barren:* deficient, depleted, bleak, austere,

bereft, drained, destitute, empty, exhausted, futile, harsh, hopeless, impoverished, ineffectual, lacking, lonely, simple, unavailing, unproductive, vain, vacant, without, wanting.

If you then plug any of those words in place of "barren" into the scripture, along with this new definition of "keeping house," this verse in Psalms adds reason and poetry to our lives: "He maketh the barren (depleted, exhausted) woman to keep house (create a nourishing place for a family to live and love) and to be a joyful mother of children. Praise ye the Lord."

I do praise the Lord for the opportunity that he has given me to learn the lessons of motherhood. As you launch into this next section, designed especially for mothers with children during the most crucial years of their lives, I hope you will find something of value. As mentioned in the preface, most of this was written when I was a mother of young children myself. Each section is about things that are important for mothers who are raising young children to think about. As I went back and proofed these chapters, some written many years ago, I had three thoughts: (1) *Wasn't that fun!* (2) *How did I survive?* and (3) *I'm sure glad I don't have to do that again!* Although it is a given that not many young mothers reading these chapters will have nine children, I hope you will forgive me for diving with you straight into ours. The good news is that we had one of every kind. So you will probably see similarities to your own child's emerging personality. Because one of the biggest challenges for young mothers is always stress, the last section of this book includes twelve chapters on different ways to deal with the stressful things in your life. Each has specific challenges designed to help you make life less stressful.

Although my life has evolved through the years to incorporate different systems for different ages of children, those can be found in mine and Richard's other books. This section was created especially for mothers of young children, who are going through what may be life's most challenging and crucial era. As I have edited, I have found some pretty funny stuff that I've deleted. I've also found some pretty good stuff that I forgot I knew. Some is even good advice for myself now! I have always believed that when we say things we didn't know we knew, it is clearly inspiration from heaven.

12

Motherhood: The Greatest Career

Normally the last thing I would consider doing during a Broadway play in New York City would be to boo or hiss because I disagree with what was being said—but it was all I could do to keep my mouth shut in this case.

The star of the show was playing an aspiring songwriter who was having a great deal of trouble feeling confident about her lyrics for a new song. Finally, in exasperation, she exclaimed (in essence), "I just can't make this come out right! It's absolutely no good! I can't do anything! I might as well just quit and go to work in some day-care center!" The insinuation was that the people with the least talent, skill, and imagination should be put to work teaching preschoolers.

One of the saddest mistakes during the sixties and seventies was the misunderstanding of motherhood. For years during the furor of equal rights and women's liberation, the press and media tried to convince us that the most demeaning job that could be found any-where belongs to the young woman who is "doomed" to stay home and tend young children—that the place we used to think of as a refuge had become a prison!

The young mother, who normally would have stayed home with her children, was wooed by the excitement of a job outside the home, complete with an orderly office, meaningful adult relationships, and tangible monetary rewards. She diligently found an acceptable day-care center or suitable baby-sitter and could hardly wait to get out into the working world so that she could afford a few more of life's luxuries and not have to totally rely on her husband for support. Somehow, money and freedom from the cares of home became the goal rather than the thought that a supplemental income would help the family.

Having more than two children was a dastardly deed in those days when "zero population growth" was politically correct. Keep in mind that I'm not saying this to put mothers who work full- or part-time outside the home on a guilt trip. My mother was a school-teacher for forty-five years and did an amazing job of giving me an idyllic childhood. I merely want to describe the militant mood about motherhood in the days of my early maternity.

Even in the early eighties the mood was angry. In New York City in 1982, at a meeting of the National Council of Women, probably the oldest and most recognized women's organization in America, I heard a young woman, Elizabeth Nichols, author of *The Coming Matriarchy*, speak to a large group of prestigious women. She suggested that the future family would be "rotational," meaning that not only mothers and fathers but also children would rotate from unit to unit until they found satisfactory settings for particular times in their lives. She said that food preparation would be referred to as almost a thing of the past because of all the modern computerized conveniences; thus, a woman could spend much more time working outside the home. "When the woman is granted equal financial rewards for her work," she said, "then she will have her own financial base and at least she will be able to marry for love instead of money."

I stirred uneasily in my seat and looked around to see if I could read the faces in the room. *Do they really believe that?* I thought as I saw a few nods, a few raised eyebrows, but mostly inscrutable stares.

Growing more and more apprehensive as time went on, I heard other speakers say such things as, "The greatest need in America today is for quality, twenty-four-hour-a-day child-care centers so that mothers can be free to work day or night." I began to wonder if our society was working to live or living to work.

The theme of the conference was, "Women and Work: Families and the Future." But so much was being said about women and work, and so little about real families. I was anxious, partly because that very afternoon, in front of this same noble body of women, I was to give a two-minute response to a special citation I had been selected to receive. I was one of six women under the age of thirty-five who was being cited for outstanding achievement in their careers. The careers of the other five recipients spanned from treasurer of the United States to publisher of *Harper's Magazine*. My award, as nearly as I could tell, was being given for my bearing and teaching children.

The statement I was going to make, which Richard and I had carefully worked out just a few hours before, was the exact opposite of what had been said up to that point.

That afternoon, at the moment my name was called, I was terrified. I believed what I had to say, however, and say it I would. As I stood listening to the person reading my citation, I took heart a bit when she came to the part that said, "She is the mother of seven children." An audible gasp and a buzz went through the audience that prevented the reader momentarily from continuing. I saw many smiles and several looks that seemed to say, "You must be from Mars." Still, I could not tell if the smiles were of amusement or encouragement, and when the reader had finished and I had received the citation from Governor Cary of New York, I stepped to the podium and said the following:

"I feel today a little like a three-year-old boy that I observed on a busy London street a couple of years ago. His mother was reprimanding him, tugging him along by the arm, and the boy was crying and protesting. I quickened my pace and, as I got within earshot, heard the boy say, 'I didn't did it, Mom. I didn't did it.' The mother reached full agitation, picked the boy up to eye level, and roared back at him: 'You didn't *do* it!' The little boy stopped crying, looked wide-eyed at his mother, and said, 'Then who did?'

"Today, in the presence of such outstanding women, I am saying to myself in the words of that little boy, *I didn't did it—didn't do anything worthy of such an honor.*

"I am, however, pleased to accept this citation in behalf of the many women who, as the program says, make contributions under relatively obscure conditions—particularly those women who make their main contribution as mothers, as cultivators of America's next generation.

"You know, all of us here, whether conscious of it or not, have multiple careers. We are all involved in more than one thing. In some careers the bottom line is profit. In others it is productivity. Those of us who write have a bottom line of publication, and in the arts we like to think we aim at perfection. In teaching, the bottom line is pupils and preparedness. But there is another career, and I think it is the most demanding and multi-faceted career of all, in which the bottom line is people—little people—our children.

"We have embarked, my husband and I, over the last few years, on an effort to popularize parenting. Our work at the White House, our writing, and our national network of parents' groups have aimed at helping people realize that our most significant and serious problems, both personal and societal, have their roots in our homes, and that parenting, when it is pursued seriously and thoughtfully, is not only life's most important career, but its most joyful and fulfilling career. Thank you."

The response was overwhelming. The audience came alive. Their enthusiastic applause told me that they had believed what I said, or at least had wanted to believe it. I suddenly realized that this audience was not hostile. Most of them were mothers who secretly wished that someone would validate their role and say something positive about families. Most knew that mothering is a career—the hardest and the best!

In a reception line afterward many clamored over our two oldest children, who were with us, and warmly and sincerely congratulated me. I felt that, through me, they were congratulating all of you—you dedicated mothers who have devoted your lives to a career at home rearing a family, regardless of whatever other career you may have.

I love to think that C. S. Lewis agreed. He said: "[Homemaking] is surely in reality the most important work in the world. What do ships, railways, mines, cars, government, etc. exist for except that people may be fed, warmed, and safe in their own homes? . . . [The home-maker's] job is one for which all others exist" (*Letters of C. S. Lewis*, ed. W. H. Lewis [New York: Harcourt, Brace & World, 1966], p. 262).

In a CBS radio interview taped during National Family Week one November, the interviewer, who had heard me expound on the importance of viewing motherhood as the greatest of all careers, asked, "Do you mean to say that you'd rather be at home with your kids than to be president of IBM?"

Although I'd never pondered that question, I felt sure of my unequivocal yes.

Managing a home and family is no less demanding or time consuming than running a large corporation or pursuing any other career. The most successful homes are run by mothers who take their careers as seriously as any top executive. However, instead of dealing with making a product profitable, we deal with making profit of human lives.

It is true that we acquire children in a different way than we would acquire a company. And we are amateurs at the business of parenthood. One morning we wake up with a pink, wrinkled little bundle beside the hospital bed and, presto, we are parents!

However, as stated earlier, the development of lovely, joyful, responsible children doesn't just happen accidentally, any more than a successful corporation just happens. A unified, organized, progressing family requires a unified, organized, progressive plan! Setting goals and producing a plan are just as essential to a mother and father as to a good company.

Just as it takes a goal and plan to become a good tennis player or pianist, and then time and dedication to the plan and concentrated effort and practice, so it is with being a good and happy mother.

And just think of the rewards—and the results!

More Challenging Than We Could Have Known

Years ago I heard the story of a wise king who wanted his people to understand the essence of life. He called together all his wise men and charged them to go out into the world and bring together the things that would most help his people to understand life. This they did with fervor, as they loved their king and wanted very much to please him.

After some time, they came back with eight volumes of carefully thought-out material that they proudly presented to the king. "Oh, my, no," exclaimed the king when he saw the volumes. "This is much too complicated. My people will never take the time to read all this! Simplify this and bring it back as quickly as possible."

Once again the wise men strove to please their king and, within a month, condensed their work to one volume, which was proudly delivered. With regret the king again reported that the volume was much too long and must be condensed. "I only want the very essence," admonished the king as the dejected wise men again set out to accomplish their task.

After much struggle they returned to the king with a one-page document, which once again was rejected as still too complicated and diversified. "I need something that even the simplest souls can understand," the king reminded as they trudged off to give it one more try.

A week later they presented the king with a scroll that contained only one sentence, and were overjoyed to see the king's wide smile as he read the statement, looked up, and said, "This is it—the essence of life in common, everyday language!" Looking reverently at the paper, he read it to his subjects. It said, "There Ain't No Free Lunch."

So also is the essence of motherhood: It's hard! In fact, it is harder than any of us could have guessed.

As I gazed into the eyes of our seventh child, only twenty-eight days old, I couldn't help but feel the same awe I had felt with the first and with every one in between. It was just at the point in time when the glaze was beginning to clear from his eyes and he had stopped seeing the angels and started seeing us.

Yes, I think *awesome* is the word to describe this fresh, new spirit, so sweet and clean despite the spewing out from both ends of the awkward, cumbersome body. He was awesome also because of the things he represented. I knew then, however—with this seventh child much better than I had with the first—what to expect.

I have to smile when I look back on those rather naive times most of us have before we become mothers for the first time. Oh my, the daydreams I used to have!

What fun it will be, I used to think, to have someone call me Mommy. How exciting to sew dresses for my little girls and knickers for my little boys, and how terrific to have a real excuse to leave a boring church meeting! How wonderful to have the family play musical instruments together, each on his own part! My list of exciting things about having a family of my own went on. *Just think of the lovely furniture, the rooms neat and orderly, and the gourmet meals I will prepare*, I mused.

When that first sweet baby finally came, I suddenly realized some things I hadn't thought of before. She had to be fed every two or three hours. I worried constantly about whether or not she got enough to eat because she cried before *and* after I fed her. She certainly eliminated the time I could spend with my husband and friends, because I was up all night feeding and changing. I felt like a zombie in the morning—irritable and grouchy.

The sacrifices changed, but they never ended as the child grew. As two more children joined the ranks, I realized that sewing little dresses was not exactly the bliss I'd envisioned. While I tried to sew, the baby screamed, the two-year-old dumped the pins on the floor every fifteen minutes, and the four-year-old cut up the pattern pieces I wasn't using.

Not only that, but as the children grew old enough to begin music training, those dreams of chamber music were clouded by the fact that the end result required endless hours of getting up early, of training the children to practice, and developing patience while living with battered ears. We went through years of screeching violins and of big tears splashing on the piano keys because, to quote Shawni, "I don't get this!" or, to quote Saren, "Oh, Mom, why do I have to practice?"

Visions of a spotless house with the beds always made and the bathroom taps always polished melted into the realization that getting children to "think orderly" was one of the greatest challenges of my life. I found that it takes concentration and commitment to get things done in the morning.

As I struggled out the door to run an errand with three little ones stumbling all over each other, and noticed the mud, toothpaste, and play dough all over the bathroom taps, sink, and walls, I remember thinking, *Thank goodness for "selective neglect!"*

I found that the laundry never ends and the kitchen always

needs to be cleared and cleaned, no matter how many times a day it is done.

I realized that the kids wouldn't eat the gourmet meals I fixed. A typical reaction to slaved-over hollandaise sauce was, "What is this yucky stuff?" Often, in exasperation, the next night's menu always included fish sticks and macaroni and cheese.

As the table became more crowded with bodies, the visions of peaceful meals—beginning with a quiet devotional, followed by each person talking about his day or something interesting he found or saw—faded into the realities of an argument about who sits where, and the wailing of the three-year-old under the table because she didn't *want* to eat her dinner before she had her a Popsicle. Somebody was always crying about an "accidental" elbow in the ribs or mourning over spilled milk.

The grand idea of every child being perfect as a result of great training crumbles a bit when your six-year-old, with a fascination for scissors, shows up with six pairs he confiscated from the school supply. (He's already used them to cut little brother's hair.) Hope deteriorates further when the three-year-old takes his friend into his room to "play" and comes out half an hour later having methodically torn off the wallpaper in hundreds of pretty little pieces as far up as his small hands can reach.

I also didn't realize that motherhood would include listening to the delighted squeals of an eighteen-month-old and a three-year-old in the back of the station wagon, only to look into the rearview mirror and realize that their delight came from watching the newly purchased bushel of peaches bounce and spatter down the freeway as they popped them one by one through the opening in the rear window.

I would never have dreamed that some day I would be stupid and careless enough to forget to take the keys to my car when I dashed in the grocery store to grab a gallon of milk. I nearly had a heart attack when I realized that my check out lady was chasing my car across the parking lot with our three-year-old at the wheel and our delighted eight-month-old as the passenger.

The Perils of Pauline could not compare to the exciting life of an everyday mother.

Truly, there ain't no free lunch!

More Rewarding Than We Could Have Imagined

I gazed at the wriggling baby in my arms, thinking about what a long, hard day it had been. My back ached, and my head pounded from a gueling day of feeding, washing, and refereeing; but I realized as I looked into those eyes that even though mothering was different than I had envisioned, it was *better!*

I relaxed, settled back a little, closed my eyes, and remembered that life is not one exhilarating joy after another. The occasional flashes of real joy, however, make us able to chalk up the rest to experience.

Who can explain the feeling of sheer joy that comes from watching a baby's first breath? Suddenly all the discomforts of nausea, the awkwardness of getting in and out of cars, and the inconvenience of not being able to tie your shoes or even see your feet, of having grown out of all your clothes and wondering if you'll ever look normal again, fade into the joy of having brought a new person into the world.

The satisfaction, much fuller than you could have known, comes when you see two little girls, obviously feeling beautiful, skipping off to their dance review in the costumes you've made (with their help).

What fun it is to see your two-year-old finally fold his arms and sit through the family prayer almost to the end—quietly—and to watch your three-year-old actually try to draw his rendition of Jesus during church services and to know that, at least for a few minutes, his mind was in the right place!

How exciting it is to hear Daddy say to your oldest daughter one morning after her violin practice, "My gosh, Saren, was that you? I thought the radio was on." Then to see the proud yet humble little smile as she realized that he really meant it.

The wonder and great feelings of satisfaction that come *because* of the struggle are beyond description. I am still sometimes overwhelmed when, once in a while, I see my two kids at home ready for school, with teeth brushed, beds made, practicing done.

Then there's the occasional meal when everything goes right. After a meaningful family prayer, everyone explains his happy day, and no one cries over the spilled milk.

What satisfaction there is in seeing your six-year-old understand repentance a bit better as he takes the confiscated scissors back to his teacher and, after a full three minutes of silence, manages to say, "I'm sorry, will you forgive me?" How great it is to see the relief— and yes, even joy—in his face as he walks to his desk with a little smile, the weight of the world obviously lifted from his shoulders.

It seems that the blessings of motherhood never cease (I guess because the hard times never do either), and the joy is so much more than we could have expected.

The effect that our mothering has is also more long-term than most of us would imagine. I cite the example of one brave colonial woman:

> One of the most remarkable examples of the sphere and influence a mother has is the life of Sarah Edwards, the wife of Jonathan Edwards, a minister and early colonist. Sarah raised eleven children while her husband busied himself with writing and ecclesiastical duties, becoming the famous one of the family. She stayed in the background as a homemaker—valuing each child's individuality and intelligence, educating both sons and daughters, but also teaching them to work responsibly. A genealogical study later tracked down 1,400 of the descendants and compared them to another family who were notorious for criminality and welfare dependency. The Jukes family cost the State of New York a total of $1,250,000 in welfare and custodial charges, while the Edwards descendants boasted the following: 13 college presidents, 65 professors, 100 lawyers and a dean of an outstanding law school, 80 holders of public office, 3 U.S. Senators, mayors of three large cities, governors of three states, a Vice President of the U.S. and a controller of the U.S. Treasury, not to mention the countless numbers who

were successful in business and the arts. Only two of these 1,400 were 'black sheep,' which eloquently testifies to the power of one great woman. (Elisabeth D. Dodds, Marriage to a Difficult Man: The "Uncommon Union" of Sarah and Jonathan Edwards [Philadelphia: Westminster Press, 1971], n.p.)

The Refiner's Fire

I had an intriguing opportunity to go through a pottery factory quite a few years ago. The pots—beautiful creations of many lovely earthen shades of clay, with graceful and varied shapes and curves—were interesting to see before they went to the firing process. In fact, they were so lovely just as they were that I asked a craftsman nearby, whose hands were the same color as the pots, why they needed to be fired.

"Oh, dear," he replied, trying not to show his disdain for my ignorance, "if we didn't fire them, they would fall apart very quickly. The least bump, not to mention time itself, would simply crumble them away. The firing makes the pots strong and durable and so much more beautiful, inside and out." His eyes gleamed as he held up a fine example.

How true this is of motherhood! We start our mothering careers as rather ordinary-looking clay pots with varied shapes and curves, and march directly into the refiner's fire.

Of course, a fire can either give luster and depth and strength or it can burn and destroy. How well we use the heat is the key.

Lately I've had a chance to see several close friends whom I hadn't seen since high school or roommate days—before any of us had children. I see in them now, many children later, a special luster—something almost indescribable, but I know that it comes from the refiner's fire of motherhood.

We can feel the fire making us more patient and understanding in spite of ourselves. We can learn to handle impossible situations with a smile. We can begin to understand the pure love of Christ as we love our husbands and children in spite of their "difficulties."

I sat in a women's meeting not long ago, enthralled with the things that were being said. The music was heavenly and the spoken word uplifting and inspiring. I felt my spirit climb to a higher realm and I was so proud and happy to be a woman, especially a mother. Tears welled up in my eyes and a lump in my throat as I realized the majesty of what I was struggling to become. The voices and faces of a beautiful women's chorus thrilled me as I watched the light in their eyes.

As I drove home alone that evening, I promised myself that I would stay in that higher realm. I felt real joy as I realized that the children were progressing, and I felt excited about some things I could do for all of us that would help to keep us in that realm.

That night, the baby woke up twice, and our two-year-old wet the bed so thoroughly that the bedding had to be completely changed. Already tired when I got up the next morning, I faced the reality of a hectic schedule that included church meetings, car pools, a guest for dinner, spelling homework with a child who never remembered, and a toothache. By late afternoon I had realized how easily that higher realm could be eclipsed by the mundane survival of the fittest.

We have to make very conscious decisions about *how* to remain in the higher realm, or dreams become disasters and life lives us instead of vice versa. The fire begins to destroy rather than refine. We must never lose sight of our dreams—even though we may reach them by way of a different path than we had expected. We can learn to expect the inevitable disasters and disappointments of daily living with children. Instead of letting them destroy us, we can learn to make them tools for a triumph next time around.

13

The Significance of Spirituality

What a revolution has occurred in the past fifteen years concerning spirituality! When Richard and I first began publishing with national publishers more than twenty years ago, we were constantly being asked by editors to "take out the parts that referred to spirituality." We had to be very careful with any reference to God or angels or prayer or divine intervention. Because we felt that our lives were guided by spirituality, it was a difficult task to say what we meant without stepping on any toes.

About ten years ago, the same publishers could see that the spiritual temperament of the world was changing. Many movies and TV shows were beginning to talk about angels and faith in God and a belief in something beyond death. Our publishers "changed their tune" and started saying, "Do you think you could put a little more spirituality in this next book?" We were delighted to comply. Recent polls indicate that 95 percent of Americans believe in a higher power (George Gallup and Michael D. Lindsay, *Surveying the Religious Landscape* [Harrisburg, Penn.: Morehouse, 1999], p. 23). Because a loving God is central in our family of devout Christians, the next four sections explain how spirituality has impacted our lives, why it is important, and how to use it as an anchor in raising a joyful family.

Life Is Fragile—Handle with Prayer

Prayer is the key to many things. It can give us peace and calmness of heart and mind. It helps us to make hard decisions, especially if we make our own decision first and then take it to the Lord for a confirmation—rather than expect him to make the decision for us.

Prayer can help us resolve dilemmas and overcome bad feelings toward others, and it can guide us in our relationships with husbands and children. Jesus has told us over and over in the New Testament that he is anxious to help us if we will but ask!

I was struck with the beauty and meaning of an original oil painting in one of the cathedrals we visited in England. It was the often-reprinted painting of the Savior, standing in his glorious light, knocking at the door. As I viewed the original painting, I noticed for the first time that there was no doorknob on his side. The person on the other side had to open the door in order to see the light.

Sometimes, we as mothers have experiences that give us glimpses into the feelings of the Savior as expressed in this painting. I had one such experience on a Sunday morning—Mother's Day, in fact. I realized as I was running the bath water for my two- and three-year-olds that they needed to practice some songs for the Mother's Day program at church later that morning. The songbook, however, had been left in the car the night before.

I'll just quickly slip out to the garage and get it, I thought as I scampered across the kitchen, still in my old white nightgown, and closed the door behind me to keep the house warm. I could hear fifteen-month-old Josh, who had followed me as far as the door, complaining about being left inside. He fiddled with the doorknob as I rummaged through the car for the songbook. After a couple of minutes of searching through suitcases, dirty clothes, and Styrofoam hamburger boxes, I laid my hands on the songbook and went running back to the door, only to bash my nose as my momentum was stopped with a bang.

With horror, I realized that the baby's fascination for pushing buttons had carried through to the doorknob, and I was locked out. I could hear him still shuffling around in the hall, but no matter what I said, he just couldn't figure out how to turn that knob without at least one lesson from someone on the same side of the door.

Dying at the thought of running around our well-exposed house in my "lovely" nightgown, I had almost decided to try to communicate through the closed door until Daddy got home from his meeting in about half an hour, then I remembered that I had left our two little girls in the bathtub—with the water running.

Swallowing a big lump of pride, I took a long breath and tiptoed swiftly out of the garage door, around the house, onto the balcony, and to the bathroom window, which had the kind of glass you can't see through. For some reason, it seemed that if I tiptoed, people wouldn't see me. I could hear the water running full blast and the children's voices.

"Saren," I called gingerly to our oldest daughter (the three-year-old), trying not to speak loudly enough to call any attention to my presence from the neighbors. No response. The running water was too loud. "Saren," I yelled, louder and louder until it reached an almost scream. At last she recognized my voice.

"Mommy!" she shouted. "It's getting hot!" *Just what I wanted to hear!* I knew she didn't know how to work the knobs on the tub. In horror all I could think to say was, "Get out of the tub."

"I can't hear you," she kept saying through the thick, frosted window.

Casting all modesty to the wind, I yelled louder and louder: "Get out of the tub. *Get out of the tub!* GET—OUT—OF—THE—TUB!"

I could feel the neighbors' kitchen curtains parting behind me, but I didn't look around and wave. I just clutched my nightgown, which the breeze was whipping around me, a little tighter and started yelling, "*Come and open the balcony door.*"

After several more "I can't hear you's" from Saren and screams on my part, I finally heard her paddling to the sliding glass door. I had heard two-year-old Shawni giggling about all the commotion, so I knew she wasn't in distress—yet. Only a few more seconds and I would be able to pull her out of the rising water.

As Saren reached the door in her birthday suit, dripping from head to toe, I began to explain how to open the door and realized that my trial was not yet over. That door was almost always unlocked; she had never tried to open the lock on it before. Pushing the lever in the right spot was a fairly complex maneuver for a three-year-old.

I tried to remain calm and explained over and over just how to open the door. After what seemed like an eternity, she at last hit the right spot and, in a flash, the door was wide open. I threw out my arms and picked up Saren on my way into the bathroom, where we found Shawni shoulder deep in water, enjoying her toy boat bobbing at almost nose level, with the water pouring down the overflow valve. The baby toddled in to see what all the commotion was, and we all just giggled with relief.

As I sat on the toilet, holding one little girl on each knee, the picture of the Savior holding the light at the closed door with no handle flashed back into my mind. How desperately he must want to get in and help us with our trials and warn us of dangers if we would only open the door! Until we do, he is helpless because he will not force his will upon us.

Prayer is a vital way for us to ask for guidance and help and to offer thanks and love. It is also a beautiful way to help our children realize how much we love and care for them and how totally we trust in a loving Father for their welfare.

As our children have grown older, and almost every child has ended up leaving for school at different times, we have found it fun to use words they can identify with to motivate them. Just before each child walks out the door, he or she yells, "Huddle!" This means that whichever parent is available takes a moment by the door to offer a word of prayer on the child's behalf, with arms around shoulders or waists. If two high school kids leave together and both parents happen to be present, it makes an even better "huddle." The prayer usually contains a quick request for safety and protection as well as help in thinking clearly during tests and looking for those who need help. Going without a quick huddle to your younger kids, who are now in middle and high school, is like going out in the dead of winter without a coat (which, unfortunately, has been known to happen).

One day after our huddle with two high school kids, we got a frantic call. Our tenderhearted freshman, Talmadge, was crying and urging us to hurry to the school because our junior, Jonah, had been hit by a car while running across the street. Hours later, after a ride in an ambulance—which contained Jonah with bones protruding from one leg and three of four ligaments destroyed in the other leg—and an excruciating period of not knowing whether there was going to be permanent brain damage, we could have doubted the effectiveness of our morning huddle. But in looking back over the details of the events, intervention from heaven was hard to deny. He had been hit directly on his legs by a car going forty miles per hour. His forty-pound backpack had been just heavy enough to direct his body straight through the windshield into the unsuspecting lap of a sweet Hawaiian lady on the passenger side of the car. She comforted him until the ambulance arrived. There were stitches to the face but no permanent head or brain damage. In my mind, Jonah was accompanied by a guardian angel that day . . . as well as by those earlier pleas for protection. Answers to prayers become so real.

I once heard Mrs. Norman Vincent Peale speak on the subject of bringing spirituality into our homes. She related a very touching practice from her own home. She said that ever since her children had been old enough to be away from her during the day, she would say to them, "What time is your field trip?" or "What time is your test?" They knew she asked those questions so that she could pray for them at those precise times. Several incidents were cited wherein those prayers had been answered. "Now," she said, "when I go to make a speech or to fulfill a special assignment, my children say to me, 'Mom, what time is your talk?'"

To me it seems that prayer is more important to a mother of

young children than almost any other single thing. I once asked a young mother to pray three times a day for one week and then to report to a women's group the following Sunday on the difference it made. She was full of enthusiasm when she reported. She said she had been so much more calm and understanding with her children. "Our home was a much happier place to live in!" she said. Then, almost as an afterthought, she added: "It's one of the hardest things I've ever had to do—to find time to talk to the Lord amidst daily demands. Boy, am I glad that week is over!"

Mothers would all admit that it is really hard to find time to pray—especially when you're awakened by the baby crying, or by your three-year-old Annie-look-alike singing from her room, "Please won't you come get your baby—maybe?" Sometimes the only way is to pray while you are doing the dishes, or to offer a quick prayer requesting needed strength and endurance just before the kids get home from school.

Not only is prayer on your own and with your husband vital, but so is praying with your children, collectively and individually. It seems we often agonize with a child about a problem at school or with friends, and then finally, as a last resort, pray about it and receive an immediate answer. My typical reaction is, "Now, why didn't I think of that in the first place?"

Some of the happiest experiences in our family have revolved around prayers that were answered: from the prayer of a lost child to find his way home to prayers for sick brothers and sisters or pets.

Prayer can improve our attitudes, expand our understanding, enlarge our capacity to endure, and inspire our minds—if we will only let it.

Time for a New Baby? Phone Home!

I don't know how mothers survive without help from above—especially when there are so many crucial decisions to make that determine the direction of a person's life. The most comforting thought I have is that the Lord is really there. It amazes me sometimes to realize how close and ready he is to help in times of need. My greatest challenge comes in accepting and agreeing with the answers he provides.

The following story is one of the greatest learning experiences of my life!

The Reservation

I could feel it coming on. The baby could get around on his own pretty well, and I felt wonderful. The other four children, although they had their individual ups and downs, were basically secure and happy. Their piano practicing was becoming more regular because I had finally gotten behind it a little more consistently. And, with the baby just beginning to walk, I felt wings of independence and a sense of joy in watching the children grow and relate to the world around them. What worried me was the nagging feeling in the back of my mind that it might be time to have another baby.

I quickly reminded myself of the many times I had thought when the last baby was tiny, "Now, remember, remember, *remember* how hard it is to have a new little baby! It takes all your time and attention. You never get enough sleep because you're up twice in the night with the baby, and then of course there's no hope for a nap during the day with a two-year-old and a four-year-old in the house, both ready to 'search and destroy' at any moment. You're so tired that you're a grouch with your husband and children all the time. Besides, you have to be on duty every three or four hours—day and night—to nurse the baby, so that every outing, whether it be a morning jog or grocery shopping, has to be scheduled to the minute.

"Waking every morning to a baby's cries cuts down on and sometimes eliminates your time with the scriptures and makes it much harder to have morning prayer. And it's a never-ending race every morning to change and feed the baby while you supervise piano practicing and settle an argument about who gets to sit by Daddy, before you organize breakfast amidst pleas of 'Write my teacher a note' and 'Give me some lunch money.' Then you get to dress and undress the two-year-old who uses the butter for play dough as you check to see that the beds are made and oversee the getting ready for school, complete with the perpetual last-minute scramble for Saren's toothbrush, Shawni's mittens, and Josh's shoes. Finally you struggle to get them out of the door with a smile pasted over your gritted teeth and a 'Have a nice day.' Next you try to help Saydi get her shirt on frontwards for nursery school while talking on the phone to someone with a problem, while fishing the cat out of the toilet where Saydi has put him to try his luck.

"You just don't have time for another baby!" I told myself over and over, to help me remember how lovely the comparative peace of routine was becoming.

Our family was just going into the third year of the greatest opportunity of our lives. My husband and I had taken a three-year leave of absence from our business to serve in London as ecclesiastical leaders to about two hundred missionaries from our church. It had been a marvelous and spiritually enriching experience. We were not, however, without challenges. It was our responsibility to feed mobs of young men and young women who had also devoted their lives for a time to church service. We regularly spoke at conferences, prepared our home for meetings, and served dinners to church authorities and members of Parliament alike. This "business" kept me hopping.

With each baby I had always been thoroughly excited about the prospect of having a new child join our family. We had been married eight years and had five children. Saren, seven; Shawni, six; Josh, four; and Saydi, two-and-a-half, had come with us from America. We had been blessed to have one child born in England—our little British boy, Jonah. My hesitation this time caused me to examine my own heart. *Am I afraid after Jonah's difficult arrival?* I had experienced placenta previa with him and he had been delivered via C-section, nine weeks early. Prayers had been answered. I had been assured that it was highly unlikely to happen again. That was not it. *Could it be that I simply do not want to give up my freedom to participate in all the ecclesiastical activities of our mission?* As I wrestled with the pros and cons (mostly cons) and with the deep, dark feeling I got every time I thought about another baby, Richard, who was feeling the same dilemma, suggested that on Sunday we follow the same procedure that we had with the other children and have a special day of fasting and prayer to get an answer. We have always believed that fasting—going without food or water for twenty-four hours—clears our senses and helps us to feel closer to our Father in Heaven when we need an answer.

This time, however, I did not even want to ask. I was afraid of what the answer might be. If the answer was, "yes," I just didn't know if I could do it. However, I finally consented, with the thought in mind that maybe the answer this time *might* be, "No, not yet. Take care of the responsibilities you have now and wait." *Oh, please tell me that!* I thought.

"OK, Richard," I said in my most determined voice. "But we have *got* to have a very explicit answer and we'll have to fast forty-eight or even seventy-two hours, if necessary, to be absolutely sure." I saw him go a little pale around the mouth. After a minute he patted me on the shoulder and said, "Let's start with twenty-four and see how it goes."

Sunday rolled around and, as we neared the end of our fast, we compared our lists of pros and cons and started talking about them in earnest so that we could take a yes or no decision to the Lord for confirmation. About that time, however, the children began to get pretty noisy. Richard called Saren, our oldest, over to the table.

"Would you please take your brothers and sisters up to the play-room and entertain them for an hour while Mom and I have a very serious talk, honey?" Curious about what we were doing, our very mature little seven-year-old demanded to know what was so impor-tant before she would consent.

"Well," he said after a moment of deliberation, "we're trying to decide whether or not to ask the Lord to send a new little person to be in our family." She smiled wryly and happily herded the others up the stairs.

For what seemed like a very long time we worked on an exten-sive list of pros and cons, and finally decided mutually, much to my chagrin, that it *was* time to have another baby if we could get a confirmation from the Lord and if he would grant us that privilege once again. As we knelt down to pray, I remember feeling what I can only describe as black, dark, and numb. I just didn't know how I could possibly do it! I suppose I was hoping not for a confirmation but for a "stupor of thought" that would tell us to reconsider.

The Revelation

Kneeling across from me and holding my hands, Richard began the prayer. The minute he said, "We have decided that now is the time to ask for another little child to join our family, if that is thy will for us," I began to feel what I would describe as a bright light of peace settling over me, starting from the top of my head and spreading to every part of my body, right down to my fingers and toes. It was as though the Lord was saying forcefully, in his own peaceful way: "It's all right, Linda. This baby is what you need; I've got a good one up here—one who needs to come now and who will teach you many things. I'll provide a way to get it all done. All is well. Be at peace."

By the time Richard's prayer was finished and I had offered mine, a conviction that a new little child would join us and that all would be well was burning inside me—overwhelming, all-consoling, and undeniable. I was a new person, at perfect peace and ready for change. Most answers the Lord has given me have not been nearly as dramatic—merely nudges in the right direction and good feelings. I was so gratified for this special, sure knowledge that he was there, loving and caring and answering.

While we were still holding hands and glowing in the aftermath of this beautiful spiritual experience, Saren, who could somehow sense that we were finished, came trotting into the dining room with a happy smile on her face and some pieces of paper in her hand.

"I organized the kids upstairs," she said. "I had them all sit in a circle on the floor and gave them each a piece of paper. Shawni and I wrote the names of the kids at the top of each paper. We told them to put a big check in the middle of the paper if they wanted a new baby brother or sister." She handed me five pieces of paper with five bold check marks below the names. (The baby's check had obviously been forged.) It was now a unanimous family decision!

In the following few days, largely because of the good feelings I had about the answer the Lord had given me, I felt particularly close to him, and my mind was flooded with things that were revelations to me. I had been going along for seven years being a faithful, loving mother, having children, learning the hows and whens and wheres, but not really realizing the *whys!*

I projected myself ahead in time and tried to look at life and my childbearing years from a long-term perspective. I was startled to realize that I would have only about twenty years in which to bear children and experience the joy of learning to manage time and feelings and people, and the joy of molding lives and developing relationships that would help me to learn and grow forever. Only twenty years! At the time—as I'm sure it does now to many of you young mothers—twenty years seemed like such a long time to change diapers; visit grocery stores with fussy, noisy children; prepare meals; and endlessly bandage cuts and scrapes. I began to realize that I needed to be anxiously engaged in grasping all the joy and happiness that was there for me to find in that short time.

I began to concentrate less on the difficulties of pregnancy and childbearing and the complications of organizing life around an infant, with the heavy responsibility of having another person totally dependent on me. I began to see it all from a new perspective: My eyes were opened and, like the warmth of settling into a hot tub, the whys began to make themselves manifest.

Having another child, whether it is the second or the sixth, is a great blessing to be looked forward to with enthusiasm and excitement. I began to relish the change and the challenges that would follow, to pour my energies into this real priority, and to organize my life to do so, because the opportunity for that particular time in life comes only once and doesn't last very long. Children grow and change; so do situations; so do I. I began to relish the joy of balancing my life so that scrubbing floors and windows became secondary to watching and relating to my children and perceiving their needs before they became real problems.

I began to realize what a great blessing it is to struggle to teach a child the correct principles of life, and to make the home a great medium to do so. What we teach our children, how we mold their characters to try to make them responsible family members, loyal citizens, and noble children of God, affects not only us and them but also their children and their children's children—an awesome and exciting challenge!

As the days passed I began to realize that my body was my most valuable earthly possession because of the miracles it could perform. My body's condition, I realized, would determine how many children I'd be privileged to have—I'd better take it a little more seriously. I felt an urgency to get in first-class physical condition so that I would be *able* to bear children as well as humanly possible for me. I decided that being in shape would alleviate the discomfort of the first few and last few months of the pregnancy, not to mention the benefits to the health of the baby. I had always known it made a difference, but I hadn't taken it seriously enough in the past to worry much about it. By "number six," and with the hopes of more to come, it was serious business. I began a short crash course of physical fitness and realized that keeping fit between pregnancies was as important as during. The whole revelation was exhilarating.

The Resolution, February 6, 1999

The baby in this story is now a wonderful, grown young man who is serving a mission for our church in Campinas, Brazil, and turned twenty on the very day I wrote this. This 7-pound, 2-ounce baby boy is now 6 feet 9 inches tall and wears a size 15 shoe. Since the day he burst into the harsh lights of that delivery room in Epsom, Surrey, England, exactly twenty years ago, calmly sucking on the knuckle of his index finger, he has been a continual confirmation of the answer to our prayer. Looking into his eyes those first moments of his earthly existence was almost scary. In those deep, dark eyes, I saw a remarkable spirit, fresh from our Eternal Father, and I felt much younger than the babe I held in my arms.

Of course, we also fasted and prayed for each of our other children; and each has his or her own wonderful story, complete with joys and sorrows. But Talmadge was, without contest, the easiest baby we ever had. He sucked on that knuckle through long meetings with church authorities in England. Unlike any other baby I had ever known, he even sat quietly in the grocery cart while I piled it with hundreds of missionary munchies.

In elementary school, this great young man struggled with difficult learning disabilities. He has taught me about dogged diligence and perseverance as he has learned how to make his artistic, creative way of right-brained thinking fit into the meticulously calculative left-brained system well enough to be able to enroll in a university last year. He played basketball there, weathered the ups and downs of rejuvenating that team, and came out with "The Spirit Award."

His insights never cease to amaze us. One evening just after Talmadge turned sixteen, my strong-willed husband announced that he was taking me out on a date. He was dying to see a movie. I was tired and had a lot to do. I must admit that I was pretty grumpy about his good-natured insistence. With one last negative comment to "my Romeo," I grabbed my coat to follow him out the door. Talmadge, who I guess had been thinking a lot about dating, heard my exasperated comment just as he passed me in the hall. He stopped dead in his tracks, backed up, put his arm gently around my shoulder and, with a twinkle in his eye, very calmly said, "Now Mom, is that how you should talk to somebody taking you out on a date?" With a giggle, I changed my tune!

There is no way I could have known, those many years ago, the joy this child would bring to our family; but I'm here to tell you that answers to prayers are real! Twenty years after our apprehensive prayer, the words of that profound revelation still flash in my mind: "Don't worry, Linda. This baby is just what you need; I've got a good one for you up here. He needs to come now and he will teach you many things. Be at peace."

☼ Use Your Handbook: The Scriptures

Every religion has its scriptures that inspire and uplift. Many of you good mothers have a natural affinity for reading the scriptures. You read them every day—or almost every day— just out of sheer desire to feel their strong influence in your lives. I'm sorry to say that I am not always one of you. I have gone through several years during which I read intensely, and then again several months when I thought about the scriptures much more than I read them. At other times I have been reminded of them only on Sunday, when I realize I have forgotten to bring my scriptures to the services.

As I analyzed this situation, I found something interesting. There are particular sets of circumstances in my life as a mother during which I am diligent about reading the scriptures: (1) when I am having personal problems or there is a major crisis in our family, (2) when I have firmly committed myself to read a certain number of pages within a certain amount of time, and (3) when I have been given an assignment.

The first method takes care of itself and has marvelous effects. I remember specifically struggling to understand faith as our fifth child, born nine weeks early, lay in an intensive-care unit with a 50 percent chance of living, and when my own life hung in the balance. Those scriptures almost popped off the page at me in the aftermath of an unexpected hemorrhage and emergency delivery. They gave me hope and faith that this little infant would be a normal, healthy, and special person.

When things are going well, however, what we feel toward the scriptures amidst our hectic lives is often guilt—because we're not reading them more regularly.

In thinking over my study of the scriptures, I realize that the first time I made it through an entire volume of scripture—cover to cover, in order—was when I had been meeting with other mothers. We had committed to each other to read a certain number of pages by a certain time, and to check on each other until we had all finished.

The pressure was on, and I read. It was wonderful; I found so many treasures that I had never noticed before. Since then, when I have reread the scriptures, I have realized that the word of the Lord is really like a beautiful kaleidoscope. As you look into the scriptures there is always a beautiful new design, with intricate patterns that mean something different each time you read the words. Because you are a different person, you will understand them on a different level each time you read. Often different things stand out because of particular experiences you are having at that point in life.

The scriptures are beautiful. I have never sat down to read them, even for ten minutes, without finding something that applied to me—that day! They keep our minds soaring and our thoughts in a higher realm.

Many study classes and scripture marathons have come and gone, but the key I have found most useful is indicated in the following lines:

> If a person hears a good idea, there is only a 20 percent chance that he will actually do it. If he plans how to do it, his chances of doing so raise to 40 percent.

If he then decides when to do it, there is a 55 percent chance that he will. If he writes his goal down and discusses it with another person, the chances go up to 80 percent. If he sets a future meeting where the other person will ask him if he did it, there then becomes a 95 percent chance that he will do it.

Although our mothers' group didn't know about this study, our plans to read the scriptures certainly validated it.

Years ago, a friend of then-twelve-year-old Saren came up with a plan originally designed by Ardeth Kapp, a great author and champion for youth. Basically, it was a plan wherein the girls decided to read a certain section of the scriptures by a certain date. It involved reading only two-and-one-half pages per night, or sixteen pages per week. The girls were to check up on each other each Sunday to make sure that the quota for the week was reached.

Getting in on the fun, I agreed to read the scriptures with Saren each day and follow the same guidelines. The result was exciting. Though we had read the scriptures often as a family, I had not read much with the children one on one. It was a joyful experience! I felt true rapture when I saw the scriptures come alive in that child's mind as we read aloud each night. I was amazed to find that she understood more on her first reading than I had on my fifth.

Sometimes, when schedules didn't allow us to read together, we read separately and then compared notes weekly. It was an exciting experience—all because we were motivated! Sometimes we missed several days and then scrambled to catch up, but as long as we were on the right page by Sunday, at least we had met the deadline (even though the ideal is always to read the scriptures on a daily basis).

Sometimes, after you have a feeling for the flow of events in the scriptures, it's also very interesting to allow a certain amount of time every day for reading rather than to try to get through a certain number of pages or chapters. The riches of scripture reading make it exciting to occasionally spend the whole fifteen minutes or half-hour set aside for study time on one page, or even on one or two special verses.

It is also important, I think, to let your children see you reading your scriptures just for yourself. Try getting up a few minutes before the kids (if possible) and let them find you reading the scriptures when they trundle in with bleary eyes. Or try setting your scripture-reading time a half hour before the older children return from school (maybe while the baby sleeps). Let them find you reading the scriptures when they bounce in from school. It's bound to improve the after-school spirit of your home.

I once heard an amusing story about "The Notorious Cold Bath Mother." A young mother with four adopted children under age four said she had finally decided that the only place she could stay awake while reading the scriptures was in a cold bath. (Some people will do anything.)

There are many interesting things to read that beckon to us each day from newspapers and magazines and recipe books and novels. Yet we will be happier if we can remember to put the scriptures first—even though there is often no time to read anything else. (If you haven't read the scriptures today, put this book down and do it now.)

Share Spiritual Experiences

"Do our children have spiritual experiences every week?" Richard and I asked each other one Sunday night years ago when we were talking about the children's strengths and weaknesses. We knew there were special occasions when they had felt spiritual help, such as when they had gotten lost and prayed to find their way. "How often do they feel that special help?" we wondered. We planned to find out.

The next Sunday, after the hubbub of trying to get everybody settled at the table for dinner had passed and things were reasonably quiet, Daddy announced: "All right, children, tonight we want you all to think hard about a spiritual experience you've had this past week and share it with the family. We'll give you a minute to think and then we'll start with Saren."

Things quieted almost to a hush, and then the almost unanimous reaction was, "I haven't had a spiritual experience this week!"

"Now, wait a minute. Let me explain what we mean by a spiritual experience," I encouraged. "Sometimes it's something big such as when a sick child prays to be healed and is given health, but most of the time it comes in simple little ways—like feeling good about sharing a toy or helping me clean when you know I'm really tired. That warm feeling in your heart tells you you've done the right thing. Sometimes it's just praying for a little help with a problem and receiving a quick, sure feeling. Now, think again."

One-by-one, the children saw the light. One child recalled that she had lost her math homework and prayed desperately to find it. She had been led to an old folder where she had absentmindedly filed it. "I know Heavenly Father helped me!" she beamed.

Three of the older children remembered that they had prayed really hard for our little dog when she had had a brief seizure the day before. (Maybe she would have recovered anyway, but I discovered long ago that the faith of a child *can* work miracles.) Each reported having had a warm feeling that the pup would be OK.

Each little child thought of a special warm feeling he or she had experienced that week, right down to the five-year-old, who said, "It makes me feel happy when I say 'I love you,'" and the three-year-old, who said, "The other day ago I woke up in my bed and you were gone and I thought you were 'died,' but then I remembered you were at the restaurant and I felt happy."

Now, every Sunday during our Sunday meal, we try to discuss briefly what each child learned in his or her Sunday School class and then have each report on a spiritual experience from that week. Rick and I report, too! It's amazing to realize that, had we not taken a moment to think about them, those precious moments might have been forgotten and left unappreciated. This discussion gives the children a chance to consciously realize that they are being helped and guided from above. More importantly, it makes them aware of their opportunities to ask for spiritual help during the week ahead.

Here are some suggestions for nurturing spirituality in your home:

1. *Pray morning, noon, and night for one week*—about specifics. Include the Lord in more of your thoughts and decisions. You'll be amazed at how much help he is ready to give if you just ask. On the big decisions, make your own judgment first and then go to the Lord for a confirmation. He'll give you a definite good feeling if the

answer is "yes." You will feel a stupor of thought or a cold, confused feeling if you need to re-decide.

How can you remember to pray? Try wearing your watch backwards on your wrist so that every time you look at it, it will remind you. Have family prayer morning and evening with all the family involved for one week. Give special attention to gratitude and thanksgiving.

2. *Tell a child that you will be praying for him at a time when he needs special help.* If you have special needs, ask him to pray for you, too.

3. *Read the scriptures every day for a predetermined amount of time.* Read them (1) individually, (2) with your husband, (3) with your children, (4) with a friend, or (5) any combination or all of the above. Try memorizing one verse per week with your family. Decide on a program (time, place, method), and tell someone that you're going to do it and that you want to be checked on by a certain date. Then *do it!*

4. *Have your children verbalize a spiritual experience around the dinner table or at another family meeting once a week.*

You'll be amazed at how much these four simple things will help you to keep in touch with heaven.

14

Children Are Such Individuals!

We had just moved, and I was far away from the hairdresser I knew and trusted. Having whacked away a few hunks of hair myself, which had only made things worse, I finally called a friend and asked her to recommend someone who could cut my hair. I seldom worry about haircuts, but occasionally the situation arises when the "mop" gets unbearable; it seems to coincide with needing to look nice for a special occasion.

I called for an appointment on the only day I could arrange for a baby-sitter and found that the recommended stylist was off duty. The receptionist assured me, however, that Leetsa would do a beautiful job. When I arrived, with memories of past unhappy experiences, I carefully pointed out to Leetsa pictures of hair I liked and strongly indicated exactly what I wanted. Carefully I explained that my husband had great fears about "scissor-happy" hair cutters, and all the while she smiled and said in her very Greek accent, "I will do you a beautiful job!"

She took scissors in hand and started snipping. I tried not to gasp when I saw her cut the first chunk out of the side of my hair. I calmly suggested that it should perhaps be a little longer, but the smile remained and I'll probably never know how much she understood about what I wanted. She snipped and sheared and kept talking in her broken English about how useful it was to have twenty years of experience. "I don't like it when people don't like to try things new," she chattered. "Oh, you have such lovely hair!"

I inwardly shrugged my shoulders and decided that there was really nothing I could do, so I drifted off into my own thoughts as the hair showered down around me. *This woman*, I thought, *has not heard one thing I've said. She took one look at me and decided how she thought I would look best, and indeed, under her "skilled" scissors, that is the way I will look, like it or not.*

Having just had a discussion with one of our older girls about what was "cute" and what wasn't, I realized that this woman was like many mothers! They refuse to let their children be individuals because they have their own ideas about what they would like those children to be, do, look, and wear! Each child is a spectacular individual, desperate to be himself from the moment he bursts forth in the delivery room.

How well we help our children to be individuals—the kind they want to be—really depends on us. It rests upon how well we can guide them in the right direction without being pushy and offer suggestions without being tyrannical.

The three most important skills in producing terrific individuals are: (1) our ability to listen with our minds and hearts and our very souls to what each child wants and needs to become; (2) our ability to observe, to perceive talents and needs by watching our children; and (3) our ability to be flexible.

I was brought back to real life from my daydreams as Leetsa stuck a large mirror in my hand and beamed at me over my shorn locks. To my amazement my hair looked just like hers, except that hers was blond. It was all I could do to keep from giggling as she exclaimed how lovely I looked and said that this was just the perfect haircut for me.

I tried to be honest and told her I had learned some very interesting things from watching her cut my hair. She blindly took it as a great compliment and I left, weighing a pound or two lighter. But I realized that, while it would take me six months to begin to look normal again, some children *never* recover from a strong-willed, highly opinionated mother who thinks she always knows what's best for her child and unwittingly makes her child into "herself," whether intentionally or not.

Let's look into some specific methods for raising individuals.

Enjoying Mommy Dates

As many mothers do, I call the time I spend alone with an individual child a "mommy date." These dates range from the well-planned, elaborate kind to the totally simple, spur-of-the-moment kind. As more children joined our family I found it hard to spend long lengths of time with each child each week. Therefore, a good mommy date sometimes consisted of grabbing my six-year-old's hand on my way out the door to the grocery store with a "come on, let's talk" look in my eye.

The challenge of that kind of "date" was getting the grocery list off my mind and turning my attention to the child. Most mommy dates are good; some can be disastrous—the kind when you end up yelling at the child because he's bothering you when you're trying to decide whether or not to buy something—but there are a few I remember with each child that were truly great! One such event I remember well, because I recorded it in my journal right after we returned home:

It was a cold, crisp, autumn morning when I took my first real walk in the English countryside. The purpose was a mommy date, and my companion was Joshua—just three years old—our first little son.

With two little fingers in my hand (he liked it that way), we walked along the bridle path that begins across the street from our house and winds its way through beautiful trees, vegetation, and stately estates with expensive cars parked in front of lush gardens obviously kept by meticulous gardeners.

Our first discovery was round, red autumn berries, which Joshua, "the great observer," carried in his hot little hand almost all the way back home before he finally gave in to the urge and squashed them.

Almost immediately we encountered one nice, big, lovable, friendly dog who, for some unknown reason, was in a hurry to get home and didn't stop long to talk—and one large, white, manicured French poodle who stared motionless at us until we got to within three feet. We stopped and then I said, "Hi, dog!" He gave two ferocious barks and ran in the other direction. This startled me as much as it did Josh, and I realized as it happened that I grasped his hand just as tightly as he did mine.

On we went, and the silence was broken only by

birds twittering in the huge, dense trees overhead and a curious little boy saying (at about fifteen-second intervals), "What's daaaaat?"—intermingled with—"We—are—on—a—mommy—date" in his sweet little robot voice. He especially liked the hoofprints in the mud and took time to mention each one.

As we walked along the path we saw crowds and crowds of ivy with small green-of-a-different-color growths on the end of each shoot, many six or eight inches long—all grown the past week. The long-awaited rain had produced almost the same result as hot oil on popcorn. The earth had been so thirsty for so long—as we had just come to the end of a summer-long drought—and evidence of joy from a week-long nourishment was everywhere.

It was a true "seldom day," the first day we'd "seen our breath" in England, and as we slowly passed by the stables and each footprint, I could feel a little boy's sense of individuality as he chose the way to go and the things to talk about.

Just as we rounded the corner onto the "civilized" road again, both Mum and son were delighted to see a big lorry (we call them trucks) parked on the sidewalk, six inches from a tall wood fence and next to a quaint old barn. Directly over the fence lay a huge stack of wet straw smoldering—not steaming—in the frosty morning air.

To our delight the truck driver got out, went to the

back of the truck, and began to operate a huge hydraulic lift connected to a gruesome-looking claw-like apparatus that picked up the straw in a huge clump on the other side of the fence and promptly dumped it into the back of the truck. We first moved closer to get a better look, but the noise was deafening, and Josh carefully and deliberately backed up about ten or twenty feet, stopped, and every minute or so reassured himself by saying, "It won't hurt me!" Every time I asked if he wanted to go home or get closer he replied with conviction, "I want to stay right here!"

At last, after a long study of the subject, he decided he was ready to proceed and we wound our way back down the path-roads which I now recognized—still finding treasures to add to our collection to show the girls at home.

The sunshine broke through, and we finished our date with a wave at the milkman, a small white feather, a large gray feather, four uncrushable berries off a nearby tree, a better knowledge of what was green and what was red, three mushrooms with soft, slated undersides, and one yellow flower.

Making It Work

Although almost every mommy date has been time well spent, some have been more productive than others. Sometimes we have had double dates, which is also kind of fun if you have more than two children. To observe how different pairs relate to you and each other is very interesting.

If you think you have to plan a big trip with each child, you'll probably end up doing nothing. Keep it simple and plan something big once a month or so. Schedule the other dates into your plan each Sunday and you'll find yourself being much more consistent. Don't feel guilty about combining a mommy date with an errand. Our little children's favorite spot for a mommy date was the grocery store.

Watch your child meticulously. Some children are better than others at telling you that they need extra time alone with you. One day one of our little girls came to me and said, "Mom, I feel depribed." Further investigation revealed that she felt she had been skipped on her turn for a mommy date. In looking back, we realized that she was right. Unexpected things kept popping up just at her moment to go.

When all is said and done, the most important part of mothering is having a good, productive relationship with each child as an individual. This is also the hardest part when you have more than one little child. Some things are just impossible to teach to, in our case, "the mobs" all at once. Divide and conquer!

Looking at the World through Their Eyes

Take time to sit back and think about one child at a time. Look at the world through his eyes for a few minutes. Daydream yourself into his desk at school. Think about how he relates to his friends and his teacher. This is a hard mental exercise, but if you stick to it for a few minutes you will begin to realize why he is the way he is. Visualize how his personality is fitting in with his surroundings, and think what you can do to help. Do something special just for him.

It is so easy for a little child to get lost in the crowd. I often think of the story of the little boy who was pounding on his mother's leg and trying to get her attention amidst the hectic preparations for dinner so he could show her a bruise on his finger. Finally, after his repeated attempts, the mother stopped and, impatient with the interruption, said, "Well, honey, I can't do anything about it, can I?"

"Yes, Mommy," her little son said in an exasperated voice. "You can say, 'Oh.'" Sometimes all a child needs is a little sympathy.

One other thing to try as you look through your child's eyes is to ask him how he thinks *you* can improve. I've gotten some of my best self-improvement ideas from kid's suggestions—like this one, "Mom, I think you shouldn't talk so loud on the phone."

Kids live in a pretty scary world. They have more to deal with than bullies and being left out like we did when we were kids. Many of them will be asked to take drugs by someone at school. Some will learn to fear violence, and some will even fear for their lives. It is so important to actually tell them that you'd like to get into their minds for a few minutes. Make it a game. Ask questions like "Who is your best friend? What is your biggest worry? Whom do you admire? What things worry you at school? What was the saddest thing that happened to you this week?" Probe their feelings and take concerns seriously. Their problems may seem silly and insignificant at times, but it is crucial to listen. If they don't talk much, it is essential to probe and explore.

Just today our thirteen-year-old was grumpy and irritable. She cried over almost every word that was said and was oversensitive to comments about her hair. She even asked for a mommy date without prompting. Something's up. I can't wait to get inside her mind and find out what it is. If we don't continually think about what we can do to be on the offense we will be continually putting out fires on the defense when the problem gets out of control.

The world looks very different to your child than it did to you. You will find that one of the most fun things to do is to try to get inside and look out. I am continually amazed at what I see!

Setting Goals for and with Them

Over the years I have used some time at the beginning of each season to re-evaluate each child and his or her gifts and interests to see how they can be used to the maximum. I like to set goals in my mind for each child, and make at least one goal to do something with him or her that takes a little time and is meaningful, such as reading a book aloud together, sewing a pillow, taking a hike, or going out for ice cream.

Every three or four months I assign myself a time and a place to talk to each child individually. During this time I discuss with the child what gifts I think he or she has and what I think we could do to maximize them. Then I ask them what they think would maximize their gifts and what *they* should do to maximize them. I ask them about their goals. Sometimes we even go so far as to get a step-by-step plan on paper to help them reach their potential and meet their goal. Depending on the age and temperament, some of the children have gotten pretty excited about it. It has given me a chance to let them know I am thinking about their gifts and needs and am willing to do whatever it takes to help them.

Ever since the months before we were married, Richard and I have encouraged what we call "Sunday Sessions." Sunday Sessions for Moms will be discussed in detail in chapter 17, but for now we are talking about their application to helping children create their own goals. From the time our children were old enough to draw discernible pictures, they have each had their own Sunday Session. Sessions for three-year-olds take only about three minutes to finish. The "session" consists of them drawing a picture of what they are going to do that week (a) for someone in the family, (b) to feel closer to Heavenly Father, and (c) to be a better friend. The Sunday Sessions get more and more sophisticated as the children grow, patterned after the example you will read later. As the children got older, Richard even formalized their sessions by giving them each an hourglass so that they could see time pass as they worked.

There have certainly been Sundays that we have missed sessions, and some kids were better at having them than others; but setting goals and making plans to fulfill them is one of the best ongoing systems we have ever used.

Surviving Music Lessons

One year the piano tuner came to work on our lovely, relatively new piano, and found a set of rhythm sticks, a pair of tweezers, a small doll, a bar of soap, and a pinewood derby car inside. In utter amazement he looked at me and said seriously, "Your children don't play the piano, they play *in* the piano." So goes our life.

Music has been a big part of my life ever since I can remember. Actually, I guess I was involved even before that, because I come from a long line of musicians on both sides of the family. In addition to teaching school for about forty-eight years, my mother spent much of her early life playing piano by ear in an old-time, Saturday-night dance band with her father on the fiddle and her brother on the banjo. Her formal music education followed and has brought immeasurable joy to the lives of about thirty piano students for the past seventy years.

I used to hate those cold mornings up in my little hometown, Montpelier, Idaho, in Bear Lake County, the coldest spot on earth in mid-winter, bundled up in Mom's old beaver coat and practicing first on piano and then the violin (or vice versa) while my sister practiced the other. I remember longing to be a normal child who could just get up, eat breakfast, and go to school, and then come home afterward and watch *Leave It to Beaver*. There was none of that for us! There was no playing with friends, no TV, no after-school get-togethers before our practicing was done.

I can still remember Mother standing over me with hands on her hips, watching the tears of frustration roll down my cheeks, and saying, "Someday you'll thank me for this." She was right! I thank her in my heart almost daily when I think of the fun I'd be missing if she hadn't made me become a musician—whether I liked it or not.

As a mother of young children, I soon faced the same dilemma. After the first few years of struggling to get our oldest daughter to practice, I remembered what had taken the sting out of practicing for my sister and me in our practicing years. From the time we were eight, our parents had expected us to earn our own money for treats, movies, *and* clothes. They provided us with a way of doing that by paying us to practice. The pay was pretty meager, but if we had had a perfect practice record at the end of the week, our money was doubled.

Richard and I wondered why we hadn't thought of it sooner. A system was devised and our first two little practicers changed from whining woefuls to eager earners. We gave them their own alarm clocks and turned the responsibility over to them for getting started in time to finish by breakfast.

Not only was there a complete about-face in their attitudes toward practicing, but they were also thrilled about buying clothes with their very own money. Those clothes were suddenly put on hangers and taken care of meticulously because their owners had worked hard to buy them. It took about a month to earn enough for a dress.

We still bought them Christmas and birthday clothes and underwear (I hate to think what "undies" would look like if the children had decided when to buy them), and there were still complaints here and there, but for the most part, it worked.

I address the subject of music lessons, or any kind of lessons, cautiously because children are so different. Parents are usually too decisive or too indecisive, and teachers are as different as night and day.

How soon your child should begin lessons depends on how perceptive you are to his natural ability, the time you have to commit, and the teachers available. A good teacher can change your child's life, increase his love for music, and teach him self-discipline—a pretty impressive contribution. A poor teacher can squelch his interest and give him a bad taste in his mouth for music—pretty scary. Parents can push too much or not enough. Often we have to depend on intuition and inspiration to get us through the hard decisions.

Some teachers are wonderful for some children and devastating to others. Don't be afraid to have a long chat with a prospective teacher to learn about his philosophy of teaching. Some are geared to making students professionals. Others are more interested in nurturing a love for music as a discipline and source of enjoyment. Decide what you really think is best for your child and then stick to it tenaciously. Someday he'll thank you for that.

Our music situation may be different than most. Because I was a music education major, I taught the children myself for the first few years. I admit that there were advantages and disadvantages to that. They didn't practice with "fear-of-teacher-condemnation" in mind as much as they would have otherwise, and it took extra time and organization on my part. On the other hand, however, it saved hours and hours of running kids back and forth to music lessons, and we used that time saved to expose them to other lessons in fields in which I have no expertise.

With the complications of more children, those days went by the wayside, and we continued to search for great teachers. But I have gained a great respect for the value of teaching your own children *something*. Use your expertise and pass it on to your children—whether it involves teaching them how to read, how to cook, how to handle finances, or how to do math. I'm convinced that you can know your children much better if you understand how they learn.

In teaching my children music, for instance, I realized that it's much harder for our more artistic children to learn to read notes. I'm amazed at how much easier it is for the calculative, mathematical types to learn notes and to sight-read quickly. On the other hand, the "soul" that comes out of the artistic child is heartwarming. There can't be a better way to get to know your child as an individual. It is very interesting to see how each child tackles a problem, handles frustration, and reacts to failure as well as triumph.

One year our family "majored" in education. Throughout the years we have tried to establish a major and a minor to work on as a family. This has consisted of each child at some time during the year (not all at once) taking a class in his or her special interest. On Fridays at dinner they have reported what they learned that week, so as to "educate" the other children (parents, too) in their various fields.

It is important to expose your children to as many things as you can—from gymnastics to ballet, from computer programming to dramatics—but remember that there is only one of you and twenty-four hours in a day. Whether they realize it or not, kids would rather have a happy mother at home with them in the afternoons once in a while than all the art lessons in the world. I used to be terrified that I would miss exposing a child to something great that he or she was destined to do, but over the years, I have learned that they gravitate to their passions. All you really need to do is support and encourage them.

Some years will be harder than others. Many sacrifices must be made—especially if you have a child who is amazingly gifted or talented in a certain field. There may be a point in life when one of these interests becomes all-consuming. Until that happens, however, your job as a mother is to try to expose your children to as many of the wonderful things in life as you can so that they can have a broad base from which to choose.

Because I know music best, I must conclude by saying that studying music is an excellent learning process and a tool for self-discipline, whether your child is tremendously talented or not. (How far you go has to be between you and your child as an individual.) During one era of our lives, one of the greatest joys as a family was being able to start each morning right at 6:30 with a hymn played by our family string quartet. Hard as it has been, I can honestly say that it's worth all the blood, sweat, and tears!

Twelve Stress Reducers with Challenges

15
Twelve Stress Reducers with Challenges

Most of us start out our careers as mothers thinking we are going to be the world's best: always kind, patient, and understanding, always having hot cookies waiting for hungry mouths after school, always there to listen to the hard-luck and success stories of the day, ever listening, ever sympathetic. Then the real world besets us.

I spoke to a mother one day who was so tied up with the stress of dealing with the demands of her children, caring for their needs, settling squabbles, and resolving problems that she said she was beginning to cringe every time she heard someone yell, "Mom!"

"I can't stand it," she went on. "Every time I hear someone yell that word I feel I'd like to scream."

Speaking of screaming, another mother told me that when life became more exasperating than she could bear, she just stepped into the closet and started screaming. She would scream and scream until she felt much better. Then it was back to the light and the world. One day her husband came home while she was screaming in the closet. He immediately panicked, found their oldest daughter, and demanded, "What's happening? What is going on?"

"Oh, it's just Mom screaming in the closet," she explained. "She does it all the time!"

We all have to giggle, because we've been there. Maybe not in the closet but somewhere, screaming in our minds that we don't know how we can go on one more day as a mother! Yet we survive. We do our best to control ourselves because we know that the tension that builds up in us can negatively affect the whole family. I've found that everyone seems to get upset and irritable when I am tense and grouchy. It may not seem fair, but it's true that parents are the "sound system" in the home, and the mother is the "volume, balance, and station selector."

A young mother recently asked me how, during the most stressful years of mothering, I was able to feel calm and in control. The honest answer is: "I rarely felt that things were in control. I lived one day at a time, praying to be able to handle the next crisis." However, hard as motherhood is, there are many clear ways to cut down on the inevitable stress and strain to the mother in a busy household. The following twelve chapters all deal with ways to cut down the stress in your life. Each chapter ends with a set of challenges that can help cut down on that particular stress. Take them or leave them or make up better ones yourself. And, if you get to the end and feel as if you've tried everything and still come to those moments when you feel like throwing in the towel, remember the solution for stress attributed to Theodore Roosevelt: "When you get to the end of your rope—tie a knot and hang on!"

I've put the hardest and longest challenge to peace first. It's the one we're asked about most often and have worked on the hardest.

16

Remain Calm in the Face of Adversity . . . Seek Peace

Try to analyze your situation. Sit down for a while after a particularly hectic (but typical) day and think about what happened. I did this one day, seventeen years ago, after a wild morning, when Richard had sent me away to write. The following story will probably give you more details than you want to know! I hope it sounds as nuts to you as it does now to me.

We awoke at 6:00 A.M. to hear the baby sounding very hungry in his bed and the new puppies yipping to get out of their box downstairs. Both baby and animals had awakened us several times in the night and we could think of nothing that we would like more than to turn over and shut out the world for another hour.

After listening to the complaints for a few minutes, Richard voluntarily decided that it was his turn to get the bottle. He dutifully picked up the baby and brought the big, soggy lump in to me while he went in search of the bottle.

In the meantime, "Miss Lark" Shawni, who was always the first child up, popped through the door and jumped onto the bed. We talked for a minute about whether or not Saren was up and then pulled ourselves out of bed to plunge with determination into the adventure of the day.

With Shawni's piano and Richard's cello practicing as background music, Josh greeted me in the hall with a whining, disappointed voice. "Mom, the tooth fairy didn't come yet!"

Struck with guilt and horror at forgetting again, I tried to disguise my shame and said calmly, "Now, Josh, you know she's late sometimes. I'll bet she'll be here by seven o'clock."

Just then I noticed that Shawni was blundering her way through her Suzuki piano lesson in entirely the wrong way. I sat the soggy baby down in the hall to run and quickly correct her before it became a bad habit. I tried to be loving and positive and gently reminded her to find her book first instead of just trying to remember the piece.

By then, Saren was behind me, after having been awakened and prodded by at least three different people to get out of bed. She was a half-hour late to start her practicing and had to interrupt Shawni by asking her to stand up so that she could find her violin shoulder pad in the piano bench. After several minutes of searching without luck, I told her in an exasperated voice to use mine, and then dashed off to find Josh.

"Josh," I yelled down the stairs, "put on your shoes and come and do the orange juice. It's getting late." As he started to the stairs, I vowed to get the tooth fairy money under his pillow right then.

That same second there was a roar from a usually calm Richard. The ensuing muttering and sputtering told me that Shawni had forgotten to put out the dog and Richard had stepped in the mess with his bare feet.

As I viewed the fiasco, I realized that five-year-old Saydi was banging on my leg, and I finally noticed that she was asking something over and over. I turned my mind in her direction (with soggy baby underfoot) and realized she was yelling over piano, violin, and her daddy's moans, "Where are the paper plates?" It was her job to set the table, and she knew I'd just bought paper plates at the store.

My eyes flashed around the kitchen a couple of times, and as I grabbed the pancake griddle and started it heating I considered how nice it would be not to have to do dishes. But I couldn't see the paper plates. I directed Saydi to use regular plates. By this time Shawni was now sawing away on her violin, completely oblivious to intonation, with her wrist tucked in the wrong way. Richard had ignored my pleas for him to go in his den to practice and was playing his cello right next to us in the family room. He was playing "Tomorrow" by ear while Saydi gleefully sang along, occasionally waiting for him to find the right note.

Josh, who was working on the orange juice, was poking at it with a spoon and using his whining voice to say, "Maa-am, you said I only had to do this job until last February and I'm still doing it."

"Oh, we just decided that you were so good at it that you should keep doing it! Try to remember to take it out of the freezer the night before and it'll be a lot easier." (*At least he has his shoes on,* I thought.)

"But, Maa-am," he said, "the tooth fairy still hasn't come!" Just then the soggy baby decided that he was going to demand to be picked up, and little Talmadge, who had fallen asleep in his clothes the night before, was hanging on my leg, saying, "My—pants—are—wet!" I could see that time was getting short—we were down to fifteen minutes for the prayer, scripture, breakfast, and three hair fix-ups before the big kids had to be out the door to catch the bus. I threw the soggy baby in the high chair and took an unbelievably wet diaper off of two-year-old Talmadge. I decided to give him a few minutes to "air out" while I made breakfast before I put another diaper on him.

Shawni was by now playing her violin on a stool in the middle of the kitchen so I could help her while I got breakfast ready. I tried to get Shawni to straighten out her wrist and play her second finger a little higher. That was the fatal mistake. I forgot to praise her first! No matter what I said afterward about how good she was, she could not be consoled. She began to whine and wail about how she was trying her very best and thought she was "doing so good" and I just yelled at her.

After about three minutes of her nonstop whining, Richard called Shawni and me into the family room and told Shawni how important it was to quit whining. With reprimanded Shawni, soggy baby, and hungry Talmadge wailing in the background, I just lost it all and got good and mad at Josh for taking five minutes to find a knife to cut the butter in half with (so that we could have a chunk at each end of the table for the pancakes). I yelled at everybody to *kneel down*, threw on the pancakes, dumped the orange juice into a pitcher from the blender, tossed two squeeze bottles of syrup on the table, and threw the baby a cold pancake to play with while we had our prayer. After the prayer we all sat around the table long enough for Richard to say, "I think we should all get back to our old idea of *whispering* in the morning so that we can all feel a good spirit in our house."

Not meaning any disrespect, I pasted on a smile and let him know I felt like strangling him with my eyes. Realizing that he had no idea what I had just been through or how ridiculous his idea sounded just then, I let it go. I finally decided that the moment had arrived when I really *had* to change the baby. I jumped up from the table, told Saren to take care of the pancakes, grabbed the poor, soggy, messy baby, ran in to change him and coo at him for one minute, and ran back out just in time to brush through Josh's hair and find my purse and divide up the lunch money. I passed the brush around to the girls, who quickly picked up their things and dashed out the door. "Have a good day," I yelled as they ran for the bus. Josh was still looking for his spelling book, but after deciding that it wasn't to be found, he decided to leave without it. As he dashed for his coat he said, "Mom, the tooth fairy never did come."

I grabbed at my throat and, in a completely disgusted voice, said, "That dumb fairy! She's always so late! I'm sure she'll have it taken care of by the time you get home from school." I kissed him on the head and said, "Now run. You'll be late for the bus!" Consoled, he obliged.

I walked back into the kitchen to see bleary-eyed, four-year-old Jonah, who had slept through the whole thing, come padding in and say, "I'm hungry. I want pancakes right now."

At that moment I realized that I had let Talmadge "air out" too long. He was standing on the window seat, watching a bird in the bird feeder, and was obviously more interested in the bird than the potty.

I quickly cleaned up the puddle, flopped the baby down with a bottle, and hurried up the pancakes for Jonah while I sewed the hem on afternoon-kindergartner Saydi's skirt (which had been "hanging" the last three times she'd worn it), then dashed downstairs to see if I could find the little urchin some socks—her most diminished commodity.

As I hurried to get *myself* ready, Richard said: "Now, dear, if I'm going to baby-sit for you like this you've just *got* to get out of here sooner." Wincing a little, but realizing again that he couldn't have known what I'd just been through, I was grateful to be leaving— with or without prodding.

So there I was—writing at last—thinking how often scenes like this occur at our house, and feeling a little anxious to get home and put some money under Josh's pillow.

I hope you can identify with some parts of a morning like the one I just described. I'd always wished for a consultant to walk through the day with me and tell me what I'd done wrong. But because I couldn't find anyone, I decided to do it myself. I recorded this incident in my journal, and after reading it over several times, I discovered several things that could have cut down considerably on the hassle. I found that with a couple of training sessions, our six- and eight-year-olds could fix breakfast. In fact, they loved making breakfast. While they cooked, I worked with the older children on music. One of the "big kids" could change the baby while I got myself ready for action. I began to see that I could change many unnecessary little irritations, while others were unpredictable and had to be coped with in a certain frame of mind. To make a long story short: Things got better. It's a great exercise to analyze your own hectic mornings or crazy afternoons and come up with some ways to simplify and make things smoother.

Expect a Few Disasters

One of my favorite book titles is *The Majesty of Calmness*. There is something not only majestic but also magical about remaining calm. It's easy to remain calm when there is no adversity. What's hard is remaining calm while your two-year-old throws a temper tantrum because you pulled him off the kitchen counter, your six- and eight-year-olds argue about whose turn it is to use the new toy, your ten-year-old begs to sleep over with a friend, your four-year-old drops a dozen eggs on the floor, the doorbell rings, and your husband sits, waiting to talk to you on the phone.

This is not an unusual situation, as many of you know. This kind of thing happens several times a day. In all seriousness, I've decided that expecting several disasters every day alleviates much exasperation. If nothing else, this eliminates the element of surprise. Sometimes it even adds to the excitement—keeping us wondering what will happen next.

Decide on Calmness in Advance

Several years ago I wrote a book called *I Didn't Plan to Be a Witch*. (Don't we always think, talk, and write about the things we need most?) Because it is so hard for me, I have worked harder on the concept of calmness than on any other single thing. I am basically not a calm person. I have to plan *not* to be a witch.

One of the most helpful things to me in my struggle to remain calm has been learning to decide in advance. By that I mean that before I step out the door to "hit the action" every morning, I pray hard that I can keep a calm spirit in our home that day through the things I do or say. I lock myself in the bathroom and think through, in the two minutes it takes me to brush my teeth and comb my hair, what I am going to do *when* (not if) the crisis arrives. I decide that I am going to remain the calm center of the hurricane—the eye of the storm, so to speak—the part that remains still when everything else is swirling around in disarray. I go so far as to even plan what I will say and how I will react. I am amazed, when I am consistent about doing this, how much difference it makes. (It works about 50 percent of the time, which is better than nothing!) When I get to the crunch I can (sometimes) think for a moment and remember what to do rather than lose control.

"Overpower them with calmness," my husband has always said. Though I have appreciated his advice, I sometimes think he asks for the superhuman. However, it has really helped to pull that thought to the surface when I have felt my anger rising, about to pop out my ears in the form of smoke.

Another way to decide in advance is to spend time on Sunday thinking over the things that are upsetting in your household. When you've sorted through the general things, think of irritations caused by each child. As much as we love them, each kid has at least one thing that is a source of contention with each parent. Methodically think through each of those sore spots and decide what you're going to do about them.

For example, one child may be whining every night at dinnertime when everyone is hungry and tired anyway. Instead of becoming upset and taking it out on the other children, decide you will send him to his room until he is ready to quit whining.

Take the time one Sunday to actually make a chart that looks something like the one that follows.

Child	Problem	My Reaction	My Plan for Better Action
Janie	*Always* has little aches and pains.	I give her the feeling that I don't want to hear about it and don't believe her.	Grit my teeth and show *real* sympathy.
John	Won't get up in the morning.	I yell down the stairs for him to "get up" so many times that I get blue in the face and furious.	Give him his own alarm clock and let him be late a few times. Let *him* take the consequences.
Angie	Worries about ridiculous things and won't be consoled.	I expect her to accept my "easy" solution, and then get caught up in an argument when she won't agree.	Treat worries seriously. Offer alternate solutions, then change the subject. Don't be enticed to argue.

Practice the principle of deciding in advance, particularly for those predictable high-tension times in the day. In our home those times have been in the early morning before school and when the children have come home from school. Concentrate on ways to make those times smoother.

It took me many years to figure out how important those after-school hours are in making the rest of the day run smoothly. It is so easy to "upset the apple cart" if the mother is worried about preparing dinner or constantly running errands or car pools during those hours.

Try to prepare dinner in the morning if you have to be gone for the day. You could also try preparing it in the early afternoon while the baby sleeps, if you're home then. During those years when all the kids were home, I tried to cut down to an absolute minimum the after-school car pool or work hours so that I could spend that time talking to the kids about their day and helping them with homework.

Another approach is that of a friend, who likes to use those after-school hours just to play with her kids, or to provide some physical or emotional outlet for them until after dinner, when homework hour begins promptly at 7:00 P.M. You have to plan according to your own schedule and family needs, but it's important to remember how crucial those after-school hours are. They can so easily slip into angry episodes because of pressures on mother and children.

If you're a stay-at-home mom, don't fall in step with the brigade of mothers who form a habit of running errands as soon as older children get home from school, so that the older kids can baby-sit and Mom doesn't have to drag the preschoolers to the grocery store or the dry cleaners. Though I know this is sometimes absolutely necessary—especially to get other children to lessons and rehearsals—don't let yourself march along with the mothers whose children answer the phone every day after school and report that they don't know where their mother is or when she'll be back.

If you are a working mom, "call-ins" when the kids get home are crucial. Have your kids call in and let you know when their chores and homework are done. My mother always worked, but I felt her presence, even when she wasn't there. I knew that she'd be checking on the amount of time I'd practiced and asking me about whether or not my after-school chores were done as soon as she got home.

My sister and I have gone through periods when we've had some fun with before- and after-school hours. We decided in advance how we were going to react to situations that arose and then decided to exude a certain aura and maintain it in those high-tension hours. Every school morning for two weeks once we called each other to ask for a report on how well we had stuck to the goal. (It was fun, and the after-school hours got to be lots more fun, too.)

Laugh

In analyzing situations, Richard and I have decided that when we reach a breaking point in our dealings with the children, the best solution is to do one of two things: (1) force ourselves to become more calm and swallow the anger, or (2) laugh. Some of the most dire situations, if viewed from another perspective, are hilarious.

One night at bedtime, I remember being absolutely furious with our four-year-old, who had pushed me to the edge. I grabbed him by the shoulders and started to shake him and scold him vehemently. Suddenly he looked in my face and let out a peal of laughter. It made me even more angry to think he would laugh in the face of such wrath, and I was outraged! After another peal of laughter, I finally blared out, "What *are* you laughing about?"

"Mommy, you look so funny," he roared. And his little brother in the other bed, who had been looking on with unbelief, started to laugh too. I thought for a minute about how ridiculous I must look, and then (though I tried not to) I broke up, too. Soon the other children heard us laughing and came running in to find out why. None of us could even explain. We just laughed until our sides hurt.

Reorganize Quarreling

One of the most universal reasons for lack of calmness on the part of both child and parent is bickering or arguing. It can drive you up the wall sooner than any other single thing.

I smiled when a "model" mother of seven (herself the oldest of ten children) told us that she has to keep assuring her husband (an only child): "All that quarreling" is normal. She told us, "He just keeps asking, 'Are you sure this is normal?'"

Another mother mentioned a family that she knew in which the children were simply not allowed to argue in the home. One of the children in this family was telling her what a frustrated childhood she had had. It was very hard and sometimes damaging for her to live with pent-up feelings of anger.

On one occasion, while we were living in England, we had staying with us a church official, who was also the father of a large family. One day we asked him: "How worried should we be about having such argumentative, strong-willed children who all think they have to have their own say?"

He looked back at us with a little twinkle in his eye and said: "If you're going to raise leaders, you've got to expect them to have and to be able to express their own opinions."

Even though that has comforted me many times, the fact remains that the right spirit cannot dwell in a home that is filled with arguing and bickering.

I still remember one occasion, at the beginning of a long trip (well, three hours) with nine bodies in a big van, when Richard offered a visit to the favorite five-and-dime store when we reached our destination if *nobody* bickered. Lo and behold—it worked! We realized that it was possible!

Several years ago, Richard and I were given an idea that has probably helped more than anything else as we have tried to "keep the peace" in our house. It involves having a place where two kids can go when they are arguing. Even though one or both will inevitably insist that they didn't start the fight, we insist that it takes two to "tangle" and both are at fault. As soon as an argument "disturbs the peace" both children are sent to a place we used to call the "fighting bench." As the years have progressed, we changed the name to the "repenting bench," because that is what they go there to do. We found the most uncomfortable place we could for two children to sit together. We started with the top step and progressed to a very uncomfortable little church bench about four feet long that we brought home with us from England.

The two peace violators go immediately to the repenting bench, where they go through a little ritual. (Practiced in a family meeting before we began so they would know exactly what to do.) First, each child has to tell a parent what *they* have done wrong. (If they absolutely can't think of it, they can ask the other child—he or she always knows!) Then, before they can leave the bench, each child must say to the other, "I'm sorry. Will you forgive me? I'll try not to do it again." Then they must give each other a hug.

You may think that this is arbitrary. It is. You may think that sometimes the kids won't be very sincere in their apology. They won't. But getting the air cleared, especially with a little hug, totally sincere or not, does wonders! Not only does it take you out of the position of being referee, it also breaks down bad feelings between kids that can make them think they don't like each other. Plus, the principle of repentance is one of the most important things that any of us can learn.

One more thought: in thinking hard about calmness one week, I passed through a series of scriptures that described the voice of the

Lord as "a still small voice" (1 Kings 19:12). What a wonderful way to describe the ideal! We can teach almost anything if we use the proper tone of voice.

In conclusion, let me reiterate that consistent calmness in any home with young children is one of life's greatest challenges!

Challenges

1. Analyze your situation and come up with your own solutions for calmness. Decide what you will do about the things that really bother you that you *can* change, and how you will handle the things that you can't. This takes time and mental energy, but it is a great investment toward peace and harmony in the home, not to mention your own state of mind.

2. Learn to decide in advance. Each morning, use the time or make the time before you "hit the troops" to think through the kind of spirit you want to prevail in your home. Go through things you might say or do in a crisis or tense situation. In essence, program your mind to remain calm.

3. Spend a little time on Sunday sorting out and deciding in advance what to do about the annoying idiosyncrasies of your children. Then stick to your plan!

4. Pinpoint high-tension times during the day and come up with a plan to alleviate the sources of irritation. Ask a relative or friend (or husband) to help you keep the plan foremost in your mind.

5. Find a place for a repenting bench. Teach your children how to use it and you will release yourself from the exhausting, Catch-22 position of referee!

17

Sharpen Your Saw

When was the last time you felt as if every forward step you took was accompanied by a couple backward steps? Whether it's keeping up with the dirty dishes in the sink or the mountains of laundry always needing to be done, it seems as though that feeling creeps in almost every day.

Often we become discouraged because we feel that our relationships aren't quite right with our husbands or children, and that there are more things to do than there are hours in the day. Sometimes we'd like to throw our arms in the air and quit, but the mouths are still there to feed and the telephone keeps ringing and we just keep plugging along—sawing away with a dull saw.

Richard's grandfather was a master carpenter. As a little boy, he used to watch his grandfather work, and he noticed that after cutting a few boards Grandpa's saw went slower and slower until smoke curled from the cutting edge and perspiration dripped from the old man's brow. The boy knew that even though his Grandpa was anxious to finish the item or had a deadline for completion, he still took the time to sit on a stool and methodically sharpen the saw. Richard loved watching Grandpa's look of pleasure when, after sharpening, he put the saw back to the board and it cut like a hot knife through butter.

So are we with our everyday lives. We can expend endless hours sawing away on things that seem important—running car pools and volunteering for the cancer drive and standing over kids while they practice—without spending a little concentrated, well-directed time "sharpening our saws."

One of the keys to survival as a mother is to have a set time and place wherein you can spend one hour a week completely alone and uninterrupted. We believe that the very best day for this is Sunday—a time to rest and re-create and plan for a successful week. (I say "we" because this was a system taught to me by my husband before we were married, and I am a solid convert.) We call it our Sunday Session, and it simply means taking an hour, each of us alone, to think through and plan the week ahead.

Now, spending an hour each Sunday alone and uninterrupted may sound easy to a single person or to grandparents, but to mothers with young children, the idea probably sounds outrageous! During a workshop on Sunday Sessions, an irate lady raised her hand and insisted that what we were suggesting was absolutely impossible! "You might just as well say, 'Why don't you take the whole day off on Sunday?' Why, every minute of my day is spent bathing, dressing, curling, and feeding children, not to mention the time required to prepare the meals and clean up afterwards. We have a constant flow of relatives and friends in and out. Sunday is our most hectic day. In fact, every day is like that, except not quite so bad! I just haven't got a minute to myself," she raved on.

She continued to be very vocal throughout the workshop and indicated to us several times what unruly and hard-to-handle children she had. By the end of the class it was obvious to everyone there (but her) that she was a prime example of the need for

Sunday Sessions. She desperately needed time to sharpen her saw instead of sawing away until the board burned—with no results other than greater fatigue. When this happens, time controls us, and we begin just living days instead of making days come alive.

This planning hour is the key to your success for the week. On the weeks when something prevents me from having my Sunday Session, I find that I'm unorganized and irritable. My stress level increases by at least 75 percent. I am solidly converted to the principle that where there is a will, there's a way. Nothing you do during the week is more important than that hour of concentrated planning.

Sometimes it requires getting up earlier than the rest of the family. In our house, Richard does the dishes after the Sunday meal, which certainly gives the rest of us a rest and gives me time to find a door that will lock so that I can have my Sunday Session. It's a little easier with most of the children grown now. When they were young, however, at every other time of the week, the kids would follow me around asking questions or pleading their causes in sibling rivalry cases or asking for Popsicles or showing me their latest "hurts." But during that one hour they learned over the years that when they knocked at the door with a "crisis," all I would say is, "I'm having my Sunday Session; go find Daddy." They got the message! You may have to work to convert *your* Daddy to the principle, but when he sees the positive results and realizes he will have his share of private time, he will likely come around.

One hour may seem like a long time. "Whatever do you do with a whole hour?" I've heard many people ask. "Surely you can plan everything you could possibly think of in twenty minutes!" We have found an hour to be just about the right amount of time.

However, I must admit that some Sundays have been skipped and some have been limited to half an hour.

The following is an explanation of the procedure that I follow. I emphasize in preface to this that every mother should have her own system. Many mothers have systems that are better for them than mine would be in their situations. The following example is strictly to give you some ideas to draw from as you formulate your own plan.

I'll start at the very beginning. On the first Sunday of every year (and sometimes periodically during the year), we organize our goals for the next period of our lives. We look ahead five years or so and try to imagine what we would like to have accomplished by then. We smile as we try to imagine what the children will each be like in that amount of time, as five years makes such a huge difference in the life of a child at any age.

Based on a few five-year goals, we write down some more specific one-year goals. (Since we move quite often and we're almost always in a new situation for the summer, we always set specific summer goals when that time rolls around.)

I keep a special book for Sunday Sessions so that my yearly goals are always visible when I plan shorter-range goals. The first Sunday of each month I take a little extra time to plan the monthly goals before I start on that week. Plans become more and more specific as we get to the weekly and daily goals.

I like to use different shapes as symbols of my goals in different areas. (This is just the system I'm using right now. I've gone through myriad ideas but this one seems to work well for me.)

I've decided that I'm not much good to anybody unless my relationships with myself and with my Father in Heaven are good. Therefore I plan those goals first—in a square at the top of the page.

The circle represents my family goals. I always try to think of something special to do for my husband first, as he is truly my first priority. Sometimes the needs are apparent; sometimes I have to think of something exciting. Then I consider my goals with the children according to their needs.

The triangle represents my goals in fulfilling my responsibility to my church and those who need help. The diamond represents the goals of "the world"—my world: daily tasks that must be accomplished to keep the home and family running smoothly.

The shapes appear in the order in which I listed them. The first three are relationship goals—with myself, my Father in Heaven, my family, and my fellowmen. The fourth is task oriented. Even organizing them in that order helps, because it is too easy otherwise to get priorities mixed up and let daily demands overtake the things that are really important.

Of course, every week is very important to progress. But you have to keep in mind that even with careful planning some weeks are great successes and some are "bombs." Your chances of success increase drastically, however, when your objectives are organized in your mind.

On the following pages is a picture of a typical Sunday Session on paper. The *goals* appear in the shapes at the top. The *plans* appear on the daily chart. In other words, first you decide what you want to do, then you decide on the exact day and time to do it! Don't be discouraged when a plan for ten minutes of physical exercise at 6:15 A.M. every day is foiled because the baby was up all night. Just make up your mind to get it done before you go to bed, or, in dire situations, to do twenty minutes tomorrow.

1. Concentrate on prayer
   Individual prayer
   3 times a day
   Family prayer twice
2. Read 1 Corinthians
3. Physical exercise
   10 minutes per day

---

1. Prepare one gourmet meal for Rick
2. Take Saren jogging
3. Help 4 "big kids" get perfect practice
4. Mommy dates for Jonah and Noah

---

1. Prepare S.S. lesson
2. Take dinner to Hendersons (let kids help)
3. Call Kim and John about youth conference

---

1. Wash up-stairs windows
2. Joy School car pool (on time)
3. Buy food storage items
4. Get sheets & towels for guest room
5. Call plumber

SUNDAY	MONDAY	TUESDAY	WEDNESDAY	THURSDAY	FRIDAY	SATURDAY
	6:00 Up–Get ready!					Sleep in!
Prayer (Individual and family)	Prayer	Prayer Morning schedule	Prayer Morning schedule	Prayer Morning schedule	Prayer Morning schedule	Prayer
	6:30-7:30 Practice w/kids	Morning schedule		**7:45** Jog with Saren		Make list and divide Saturday's work
9:00-12:00 Church meetings	**7:30** Breakfast					
Teach Sunday School	**8:00** Get Saren out door					
	Give Josh music lesson while other kids do dishes					
	8:30 Take kids to school–Jog 10 minutes					

Schedule — Sunday (leftmost column)

- Prayer (Individual)
- Sunday dinner
- Sunday Sessions for everyone
- Write to Grandma
- Get kids to do letters and write in journals
- Family scripture and discussion
- Prayer (Individual and family)
- Dinner
- 7:30 Call Kim and John
- Bedtime Reading time

Monday

- 9:00 Call plumber
- 9:15 Joy School car pool / Run errands
- 11:45 Pick up kids
- 12:00 Read scriptures while kids eat lunch
- Prepare soup and bread
- 3:30 Kids get home / Talk about school
- 4:00 Cub Scouts
- 5:30 Special dinner
- 6:30 Family meeting / Family prayer
- 7:30 Bedtime Reading time

Tuesday

- 9:00 Jog 10 minutes
- 9:30 Get food storage items
- 12:00 Read scriptures / Prayer
- 1:00 Prepare dinner with Talmadge / Gourmet dinner for Rick
- 3:30 Kids home
- 4:00 Electronics class for Josh / Take Jonah for Mommy date
- 5:30 Dinner / Prayer
- 7:00 TJC meeting

Wednesday

- 9:00 Jog 10 minutes
- 9:15 Joy school car pool / Get towels and sheets
- 11:45 Pick up kids
- 12:00 Read scriptures / Prayer / Prepare dinner
- 2:30 Dentist for Shawni
- 4:40 Kids home / Homework
- 4:30 Mommy date for Noah
- 6:00 Dinner / Family prayer
- 7:00 Orchestra rehearsal for Saren / Prayer

Thursday

- 9:30 Prepare dinner for us and Hendersons (Noah and Talmadge help)
- 10:30 Wash upstairs windows
- 12:00 Read scriptures / Prayer
- 1:00 Prepare Sunday School lesson while Noah sleeps / Talmage and Jonah play
- 3:30 Kids home / Take food to Hendersons
- 4:00 Shawni's art class
- 6:00 Dinner / Family prayer
- 8:00 Meeting with Oswalds

Friday

- 9:00 Jog 10 minutes
- 9:15 Do washing. Keep at it till it's done!
- 12:00 Pick up kids and run to junior high and do sectional rehearsal for orchestra
- 2:00 Get Jonah off to birthday party
- 3:30 Mommy date for Noah—to grocery store
- 4:30 Take kids ice skating
- Dinner
- Family prayer
- 9:30 Movie

Saturday

- 9:00 Jog 10 minutes
- 9:15 Do washing. Keep at it till it's done!
- 1:00 Rick takes kids to Daddy date—store
- Prepare Sunday dinner
- Baths
- Dinner
- Family prayer
- 7:00 Watch TV special with kids

When you get your goals and plans written down, half the battle is won! It's sort of like writing down a grocery list: If you write it down and then forget to take the list, you can still remember most things when you get to the store.

Just having those goals organized in your mind is invaluable. Of course, more things come up in a week than you can possibly write down or calculate. Sometimes not everything on the list gets accomplished, but if you have a framework, and if you are sure that your priorities are in proper perspective, the advantages will be immeasurable. That frantic feeling of having more to do than you can handle and of losing control of your time will be cut to a minimum.

Challenge

There are 168 hours in every week. Take one of those hours every Sunday to plan your week. Arrange a tradeoff with your husband so you can each have your individual hour. If your husband is not at home, have older children tend the younger ones, or even hire a baby-sitter if necessary, just so that you can sharpen your saw. Plan everything from your priorities to your menus. Plan to fulfill your needs and the needs of your family and friends. Remember that it's much better to plan and partially fail than not to plan at all. Use a planning method that best fits your own family and its lifestyle—but *plan!*

18

Get Lost and Find Yourself

I'm a great believer in solitude and its absolute necessity to the effective mother. This section goes beyond the one hour of concentration time on Sunday to a few additional hours a week or sometimes an extended period of solitude.

William James described a woman's life as a state of *Zerrissenheit*, a German word that literally means "torn-to-pieces-hood." To avoid this, and to be of any help to others, we have to take time to turn our thoughts inward—to think and to contemplate our direction and our intent.

One summer, when we were able to live at Bear Lake, Idaho, Richard had a six-week assignment in Salt Lake City, Utah, so he had to spend three-and-one-half days with us and three-and-one-half days in Salt Lake every week. My mother lived nearby (I was born and raised in the area), and going into Montpelier to have fun with her, weed her garden, and get groceries provided a nice break a couple of times a week.

We had just come from Washington, D.C., to spend the summer at the cabin, and time was passing quickly. Even though it was a change, the schedule remained demanding. There were still seven little mouths to feed three times a day, a baby that still woke up three times a night, and a cabin to try to keep in some semblance of order with anywhere from nine to thirty-five bodies tracking sand and dirt and wet towels in and out all day.

Our oldest girls practiced on violin and piano every day, and I tried to do some music theory with the oldest four children every morning. The "big kids" also loved cooking something new every afternoon, and Saren, our oldest, needed to be instructed in her efforts to make her first dress.

Everything was lovely for five weeks, and then suddenly I could feel myself becoming irritable with everybody. My temper started flaring over little things, and the children's arguments and whining really got on my nerves until I felt like clobbering somebody.

Rick noticed my bad moods and asked what was wrong, but I couldn't really tell him. One Sunday evening he sent me to the beach to do some writing. I walked down to the shore and enjoyed the unending and ever-changing beauties of the lake, the sand, the mountains, and the wide expanse of cloudless, brilliant blue sky.

It made an immediate difference in my feelings. I realized that I had never in the entire five weeks walked away to be on my own. I had never enjoyed that beautiful sight without a baby wriggling on my hip, or a husband needing a boat driver so he could water-ski, or the children yelling, "Hey, Mom, watch me swim!"

At first I felt angry about that discovery, and then, as I analyzed how it could have happened, I realized that it was mostly my fault. We mothers tend to get in a rut. Most days the responsibility and privilege of caring for children is ours, as our husbands go off to support the family. We get accustomed to that and fail to realize that it doesn't have to be that way every day.

It takes a conscientious effort from husband and wife and

children to occasionally change the pattern. A mother can be a lot more effective the rest of the week if she has a few hours off to just do her own thing. Though my good husband had been wonderful to see that I got that time away while we were in Washington, our schedule had changed for the summer and we had all kind of forgotten about it.

I knew that I needed time to be alone—out of the house and away—at least once a week, but I had let myself get bogged down with always seeing that my job never ended. Somebody always needed me. Even with only four rooms in our little cabin to take care of (and the children really did most of it), there was still a hard-to-get-rid-of compulsion to wash or clean or teach or preach.

When I got to "my place" on the beach I wrote the following poem, which helped me to sort things out:

> *Lonesome*
> For weeks it seems
> I've been:
>> Cleaning cupboards
>> Cleaning floors
>> Cleaning faces
>> Cleaning sores
>>
>> Sorting clothes
>> Sorting needs
>> Sorting garbage
>> Sorting pleas
>>
>> Mending armholes
>> Mending ceilings

Mending knees
Mending feelings

Cooking cakes
Cooking corn
Cooking self
Cooking—worn

Getting angry
Getting messed
Getting dunged on
Getting pressed.

I've been surrounded by:

Arguing children
Creative children
Begging children
Laughing children
Practicing children
Crying children
Caring children
Adorable children
Others' children
Demanding children

And

Talkative friends
Concerned friends
Interesting friends
Dinner friends
Tennis friends

Drop-in friends
Book-writing friends
Knife-making friends
Farm friends
And
Loving husband
Demanding husband
Creative husband
Understanding husband
Un-understanding husband
Exciting husband
All-consuming husband.

And through it all
I feel something—uneasy,
Not really depression
or confusion, or insecurity
(but some)
I think just mostly
loneliness
How strange
—with all that—
lonely?
Yes!
Lonely for myself:
Time to think
and create
and analyze:

cleaning

sorting

cooking

getting

children

friends

husband

alone.

We mothers have to be "selfish" (or selfless, depending on which way you look at it) enough at least once a week to spend some time alone. And again, I'm convinced that where there's a will there's a way.

But often it takes more than just one hour on Sunday. On a morning that Richard was there I could have jumped up just before he reached for his fishing pole and said that I was going jogging or down to the beach to write for a while. Even better, I could have arranged it with him the night before so the fish wouldn't have to be disappointed that he didn't come. Although it seemed impossible at the time, I really could have put the older children in charge during the baby's nap and left—even if it was for only half an hour (that baby was a short napper). I could have worked out all sorts of better ways to take care of myself. I guess I just either had a "martyr's complex" or else I didn't even realize my dilemma. Even my sacred hour on Sunday had not been used very well because of our schedule change. And I had waited until I became a grouchy old bear and miserable to be around before I finally realized it.

In *Gift from the Sea*, Anne Morrow Lindbergh advocates escaping. She says:

> Every person, especially every woman, should be alone sometime during the year, some part of each week, and each day. How revolutionary that sounds and how impossible of attainment. . . . By and large, mothers and housewives are the only workers who do not have regular time off. They are the great vacationless class. . . . If women were convinced that a day off or an hour of solitude was a reasonable ambition, they would find a way of attaining it. (New York: Pantheon Books, 1955, pp. 48–49)

Every mother has different needs. During the normal school year, when I usually had three preschoolers to "play with" all day, I found that I had to get in the car once a day (or at least walk around outside for a while) to free my mind for a few minutes. There are many ways to accomplish that end, but the important realization is that it must be done.

If your husband doesn't offer, point out your need (I know that's sometimes the hardest part) and work out a deal with him whereby he can take the kids (yes, even the baby) sometimes on Saturday or Sunday for a few hours so that you can be alone. If your husband just isn't available, or you are a single mom, get a baby-sitter, a sister, or a neighbor to help. Spend your time well, and you'll be a new wife and mother by the time you return. Somehow it's much easier to bear down and work hard if you know there is light at the end of the tunnel.

We once asked a bright couple with eleven children how they

survived. They smiled knowingly, and the father said, "You know, it really is hard at times to keep yourself together with the rigorous demands of career and children. It's equally or probably even more demanding for my wife. Mary's career is the children and the household—a never-ending, always demanding career. We found that our most valuable possession was our little playhouse, just out of sight in the backyard, with one single bed. When one of us got to the point where he or she couldn't take any more, that one would say, 'I've had it! I'm going to the playhouse!' The other would understand as the frustrated parent grabbed blanket and pillow and headed for the secret hiding place. The children knew they were not to disturb that person until he or she returned."

We have used that philosophy several times in our marriage. When we were living in England, we had occasional responsibilities in the Channel Islands between England and France. About once every three months I flew down twenty-four hours before our scheduled meetings, either all by myself or with a nursing baby, and simply dove into the writing and reading I'd been dying to do— only coming up occasionally for food and a jog along the beach. The next two days Richard joined me for meetings, and then he stayed an extra twenty-four hours to write and read after I had returned home.

I think I accomplished more in establishing goals and thinking about relationships with my husband and children during those concentrated times than I had at any other time.

Another example: One year Richard went on a ten-day trip to Washington, D.C. When he got home I was fit to be tied and wondered if I was still in my right mind!

Richard could see that I was about to collapse, so he immediately called a nearby hotel, made a reservation, and sent me away with the nursing baby for twenty-four hours to spend as I saw fit. It was so wonderful that I could hardly believe it. Just before I left, I confided in two friends who happened to be with me at an aerobics class that I was going away for a whole day to be myself. Obviously, neither caught the gist of the program. One said, "Are you having trouble sleeping?" She was evidently very puzzled and secretly wondered if this was a trial separation. The other shuddered and said, "Oh, I don't know what I'd ever do with myself."

With a great sense of freedom and joy, I checked into the hotel at about noon and immediately got some sleep—something I hadn't had enough of for two-and-one-half months, ever since the baby was born. Renewed, I pushed the baby to a nearby shopping mall and spent two hours just shopping for myself, spending the Christmas money I hadn't had time to use. What a wonderful feeling!

I had time to think about the richness of my life, and think about what I wanted for the future. Best of all, when I left my pencil at my desk and went into the bathroom, IT WAS STILL THERE when I came back!

The baby thankfully slept through the night, requiring only to have the pacifier pushed back into his mouth a few times, and slept until 6:00 A.M. I fed him, slept again, got up, and washed my hair— for the first time in a week. What an exhilarating feeling it was to get just me and one other little person ready!

I went home a new woman. I had stepped back and looked at my life and at how very blessed I was! I had set goals for myself and my relationships with husband and children. I had had time to read scriptures for a while and to pray meaningfully, not just for a few minutes at the beginning and end of each day. It was heavenly!

Let me emphasize here that I realize my husband is very different from many husbands. Not every husband could or would stay with children for a whole day (especially during the week), and so other arrangements must be made. A mother, a sister, or even a neighbor might be willing to help if you asked or offered a trade of some sort. Your husband may even surprise you if you lay it all out on the table and tell him exactly how you feel. Sometimes it is hard for husbands (as it is for us) to see our needs until we present them in a rational, organized way.

Again in *Gift from the Sea*, Mrs. Lindbergh writes with great perception and clarity about solitude:

It is a difficult lesson to learn today—to leave one's friends and family and deliberately practice the art of solitude for an hour or a day or a week. For me, the break is the most difficult. Parting is inevitably painful, even for a short time. . . . And yet, once it is done, I find there is a quality to being alone that is incredibly precious. Life rushes back into the void, richer, more vivid, fuller than before. (p. 42)

Challenges

1. Find time to be alone. Get help from your husband, mother, sister, or baby-sitter. Don't say you don't have time. Make time! It is more important than almost anything that you can do to be a better wife and mother. Find a short time each week and an extended period every few months.

2. When you find the time, use it wisely. Enjoy the time it takes

to just unwind. Then use the remainder to create your goals and plans—in essence, write your diary in advance.

3. Use the renewing influence of this solitude to improve your relationship with yourself as well as with your husband, children, family, and friends. Certain springs can be tapped only when you are alone.

19

Teach Your Children Responsibility

There are many specific ways to cut down on stress in a normal hectic household. One of the most vital is to share the workload with husband and children. Although this will almost inevitably produce mass pandemonium initially, it's worth sticking to until the process becomes expected and routine. Don't despair, no matter what. As children learn to accept responsibility—from the tiny beginnings of the two-year-old being able to get a diaper for the baby to the big things like a ten-year-old doing a good job cleaning the bathroom—it is so much the better for everybody involved.

Many times we say to ourselves in exasperation, "I could do it so much faster and easier myself!" Just remember—it's worth the time and trouble in the long run to teach your children responsibility. Don't tire yourself by trying to get children to do things beyond their ability. There seems to be a certain breakthrough point (different with each child) at which a child can truly be responsible for his own things and for specific household duties. Remember that pre-schoolers should feel joy, not responsibility. We've found that little responsibilities for children are good when they start school.

Because Richard and I have written a book (*Teaching Children Responsibility*, Salt Lake City: Deseret Book Co., 1982) that goes into great detail about responsibility, I will not attempt to do that here. However, I have so often been asked about our children's responsibilities over the years that I will give a brief sketch, knowing that each household is very different (many do a better job than ours) and that each year our responsibilities change.

(Just a footnote, after seventeen more years of experience: Before you read this next section, remember that you do what you have to to keep your sanity! Having many children at home required a pretty crazy schedule. I hope this doesn't put anyone on a guilt trip or sound too insane to someone with two children, a nanny, and a housekeeper. Things are so much more relaxed now in our home. You should also know that at least two of our three current teenagers' rooms are basically a disaster.)

Typically, our two older girls would get up in time to be dressed and ready for violin practice by 6:15 A.M. They had their own alarm clocks so that I could get myself ready quickly while they began. We would usually have ensemble practice (with me on the viola and Richard on the cello) at 6:30. Then, while I gave at least one music lesson to one of them, the next two children would get themselves dressed and cook breakfast (their music lessons were in the afternoon). I would also work on hair and diapers, dress preschoolers, and help with the last-minute breakfast details so that we could kneel for prayer at 7:30 and be finished with breakfast and have the four older children ready to catch the bus at 8:00.

After school, one child would be assigned a quick "run through" on the upstairs, another on the downstairs, meaning that they straightened rooms and picked up the things that were out of place.

Another child was expected to get all the garbage gathered and put out, and another to clean one bathroom. Each child was also expected to have a clean room. At dinnertime the plates were turned upside-down, and the children were not allowed to turn them over so we could eat until their jobs were completed.

After dinner, one child would clean the table, another would do dishes, another would sweep the floor, and another would later empty the dishwasher.

Before they went to bed, each child would set out his clothes for the next day, brush his teeth, and say prayers.

We simplified all these responsibilities with what we called our "peg board." It was a three-dimensional board with four holes below each child's name, into which pegs were plugged when each job was completed. The first peg represented morning responsibilities (making beds, brushing teeth, saying prayers, and getting out the door on time); the next peg represented music practicing (when kids weren't taking lessons, this peg included reading time or homework); the third peg represented daily jobs or areas of the house for which they were responsible to keep clean; and the fourth peg represented nighttime responsibilities, which included laying out clothes for the next day and getting to bed on time.

This peg board (also explained in more detail in *Teaching Children Responsibility*) simplified the concept of responsibility in the children's minds; and when those pegs were in place, they felt a certain sense of real satisfaction (and my everyday stress and strain diminished greatly).

Let me hasten to add once again that every peg did not get put in every day, and it took a great deal of remembering and reminding myself to remind the children at first, but it did get easier!

One of the great keys to making this work is having the support and help of your husband. Although the mother is there more of the time and therefore is usually the taskmaster, a firm reminder from Daddy and frequent urgings from him about the importance of fulfilling responsibilities can do wonders.

Another valuable tool is the actual help of the father. Rick helps when he can during the week, but he always gives us all a rest and does the dishes on Sunday. This began on the first week of our marriage as a kind gesture and has turned into a tradition that the children have never let him forget.

Although I have emphasized the struggle many times, we have discovered over the years that children will do exactly what they know is expected of them. If they understand these expectations when they are young, life gets easier rather than harder as they get older.

You can make the task more fun by changing systems or rewards occasionally to keep minds and hands excited. I will not include elaborate systems here, although there are many. Use one that children and parents both feel excited about.

One of our greatest finds in teaching children responsibility came from a school near our home in Washington, D.C. Because there were not enough available mothers or teacher's aides to hear the children in the early grades read, the school solicited the aid of older students who were doing well to come in and listen for a few minutes several times a week. Our children considered it a great honor to be asked to be a "tutor." Both tutor and "tutee" loved the program and learned a great deal.

We decided to let the natural love children have for younger children come into play in our own family.

When a child reached the age of eight, a big transition took place at our house. He or she became one of "the adults." (You can choose to have this happen at any age.) The child could then attend an adult planning meeting each Sunday night, where we discussed our strategy for the "little kids" during the coming week. Every month one of the "adult" children was assigned to be a tutor for one of the children under eight. This meant that he sat by him at the dinner table and helped him with his food if necessary. He saw that his "tutee's" teeth were brushed and his bed made, and he acted as a partner on excursions to the zoo or shopping.

There is nothing more fun than watching a nine-year-old try to help his three-year-old tutee to brush his teeth. I must admit that after we began enlisting the "other" adults' help, our jobs became markedly easier. Every month we exchanged tutors and tutees so everybody had a chance to help or learn from everybody else. It was wonderful to watch the growth on the part of both tutor and tutee! For those of you who don't have anybody who is eight yet, hang on—help is coming!

Challenges

1. Set a daily schedule and live it. Make adjustments when necessary, but don't let the exceptions become the rule.

2. Read *Teaching Children Responsibility.*

3. Have a "tutor and tutee" system if you have some children over eight and some under. Make older children part of the solution rather than part of the problem.

20

Expect Respect

We live in a permissive society! Sometimes this permissiveness creeps into our own homes before we even realize it.

I recall an experience I had when we had just arrived in England. Joyce, an outspoken young English girl who was helping me one day, couldn't help hearing a rather heated conversation between me and our oldest daughter, Saren (who was six). After it was over and Saren had disappeared, Joyce said to me, "Why do you let Saren talk to you like that?"

"Like what?" I asked, amazed that she would think it was peculiar.

"Like she did this afternoon when you were 'having words' with her. Americans seem to let their children speak to them in such a dreadful manner!"

I was shocked, but I've come to be grateful to Joyce for that question, because it might otherwise have taken me quite some time to recognize that Saren really did have a nasty tone in her voice when she disagreed with me. She had been speaking with near contempt. I had simply tuned out the offensiveness in her voice because I'd heard it often. But, in thinking about it, I decided that Joyce was absolutely right and that things were going to change.

"It's all right to ask questions," I told Saren that evening, "but you must remember to use a respectful tone of voice." As she grew up, she occasionally ventured too near the line, but when I gave her a certain signal, she usually remembered to calm down.

The bottom line in getting respect from your children (other than the obvious one of deserving it) is that they will give you exactly as much as you expect.

Two other vital ingredients are: (1) Begin when the children are very young. When children are ten it is too late. They must understand clearly from the beginning that there is a certain tone of voice that is not acceptable in your family. (2) Enlist the support of the father. If he is always aware of the slightest tone of disrespect to his wife from the children, one stern statement: "Don't ever speak to your Mommy like that!" does wonders.

Interestingly, when we were on *Oprah* several years ago to talk about our book *Teaching Your Children Values,* one of Oprah's favorite topics was respect. One method she particularly liked was teaching children to show respect for others by looking them straight in the eye. This is very hard for some children, especially when they are dealing with an adult; but it says a lot about their character if they can do it. Practicing looking people straight in the eye in a family meeting is fun and extremely valuable.

If children know that a certain level of respect must always be maintained in the home, the stress level inevitably drops. This is something that is easily overlooked but adds much to having a consistently better spirit in your home.

Challenges

1. Step back and listen to the tone of voice used commonly in your home. If it is undesirable, design a plan to

do something about it. Remember that kindness and consideration begin with you. How do *you* sound when you're angry or irritated? (Listen to your children when they're arguing, and—possibly to your chagrin—you'll find out.)

2. Help children learn to look others straight in the eye by practicing.

3. When children use a disrespectful voice, say, "Wait, let's start over," and then have them repeat their response a little more kindly. It may take several "start overs," but they will get the idea that you expect respect.

21

Simplify—Not Super Mom, Just Happy Mom

Simplify—what a great key this word is in coping with stress! There is a way to simplify everything. Try turning things around and thinking in terms of how little, not how much, you can get along with. The lives of most people in America today are cluttered with too many "things." Even those who can't afford them are duped by advertising schemes in the media and fill their lives with unnecessary things. Our lives easily become cluttered with "stuff."

Having fallen into the same pit ourselves, we are often glad when we are required to move from one home to the other, because it allows us to get rid of so much stuff! We can never believe all the junk we have collected over the years. There are broken toys that we kept thinking we would mend, puzzles with missing pieces that I *knew* we could find, books with torn pages that I rationalized someday the children might look through and enjoy. We find clothes that no one ever wears and "early-marriage" furniture that we finally, fondly, decide to part with.

When we used to move back to Washington for months at a time every few years, we would take less than half of our furniture with us, and we found that we got along beautifully. Our home there was much smaller, and the housework time was cut in half. When we would move back out West for the summers, each of the children would bring to our four-room cabin two playsuits, and one Sunday outfit, and life would become even more pleasant. Granted, summer and beach life required less clothing, but I was amazed to find that our trips to other places were also simplified. That amount of clothing was sufficient as long as I had access to a washing machine. (And the baby, of course, had a few extra pieces of clothing—especially pajamas.)

At one point I simplified my own wardrobe and got rid of everything I hadn't worn for a year. I cleared out my jewelry box full of earrings and got down to a basic four. (I had to have backup for when I lost some, which is about every week.)

At Christmas each child got one gift from Santa Claus and one Christmas outfit. Any other gifts were considered "cream."

There are so many ways to simplify. Serve granola bars and prepared orange juice for breakfast and super-easy cleanup. Simplify meals and cleanup on busy days with paper plates, and yes, sometimes even convenience foods. Simplify errands by finding ways to cut out those that aren't absolutely necessary, and by combining them with other runs. Simplify toys by getting rid of or at least putting away the ones your children don't love. Don't buy toys with thousands of pieces until their owners can take care of them. Give the children more Scotch tape and paper to create with. There are a thousand ways to simplify your life if you can think about it long enough to decide how.

Don't give up your favorite things to the point that you feel deprived. For example, I know that an artificial Christmas tree would save time and money at the holiday season, but I can't bear to give up the family fun of going to get the tree, or the smell that means Christmas to me. If arranging an elaborate table for dinner guests is your "thing," enjoy it—set the table and then call for Chinese delivery.

Early in our marriage I really enjoyed preparing elaborate dinners for friends (although I smile when I remember how I used to clean the refrigerator and oven and scrub and wax the kitchen floor every time). But often with the stress, I became angry and irritable with the kids because I felt I needed to do things exactly as I thought they should be done. Finally I realized that I was complicating my life unnecessarily. We simplified and started meeting friends for dinner at a restaurant, which made it so I could enjoy the dinner too.

We have also had many study groups in our home. After the discussion, a lovely dessert is usually expected, and as most of the time the group rotates homes, each wife always tries to plan something more elegant and delicious than the last. When our lives got too complicated I decided to make a pact with the other wives to serve plain water—or nothing at all. Somehow I enjoyed those discussions much more because I was not worrying about getting out the refreshments before someone had to leave. I actually listened and participated.

Don't let yourself fall into the trap of believing that because all the other mothers throw elaborate birthday parties for their kids, you have to do the same. Do something that's easy but has pizzazz. I remember crying over the dirty stairs one day two hours before a birthday party for our three-year-old because they were littered with everything from popcorn to nails. I was sure everyone at the party (*all* those three-year-olds) would think me a terrible housekeeper if

I didn't get my stairs vacuumed. However, I was due to have our third baby any day and was having regular contractions.

What a silly mother! Instead of having the party outside, I complicated things as much as possible and got on the phone and called until I found a teenager in the neighborhood whom I could hire to come and vacuum my stairs. (I guess it could have been worse. I could have vacuumed the stairs, gone into hard labor, and had the baby during the party.)

If only I had had the word *simplify* in my mind, I could have saved myself a lot of grief as a young mother. Remember the principle of pizzazz as you simplify. There is a fine line between simplifying and becoming mediocre. Use your creativity and do things with flair but in the simplest form.

 ## Challenges

1. Dare to be different and simplify! It's one of the most timesaving, stress-reducing devices you can find.

2. Start with the things around you. Get rid of the "stuff." Simplify your own wardrobe as well as the children's. Learn to simplify things in your mind when it seems that there is more to do than you can handle.

3. Cut out unnecessary distractions and don't worry about trying to keep up with the other mothers. In fact, if you simplify effectively, they might want to try it themselves.

22

Put Your House in Order

I have a confession to make. I am not a naturally tidy person. I somehow managed to blunder through high school and college, excusing my disastrous room with obligations to practice and leadership responsibilities at school. My dad used to jokingly call me "Mrs. Smith," the name of a particularly disorganized neighbor. (One day I asked to use her phone, and, after picking my way through the debris to the phone, I turned around to see their dead Christmas tree still decorated in the corner. It was March.)

At college I was "blessed" with a roommate who was exactly like me and, though we both did well in school and were gone most of the time studying or practicing, we always returned to a room that looked very much like someone had thrown in a live hand grenade and shut the door. Occasionally I'd turn over a new leaf, but it was short-lived.

It seems to me that I improved for a while after our marriage, thinking how embarrassed I'd be if *he* found out how bad I was. As children came along, however, things began to get muddled again, and I began getting up in the morning to a sink full of dirty dishes that I had been just too tired to wash the night before.

After four children and many, many commitments to try harder, I finally reached the point where I could no longer tolerate the messy rooms at night, the lost shoes, clothes, scissors, papers, and so forth. We decided in earnest that the time had arrived. All the "wouldn't-it-be-nice" ideas were to be implemented. I quickly realized that any plan had to start with me, the mother!

A good friend had taught me the principle of touching things only once, which helped me immensely. For example, if your recipe calls for salt, take it from the cupboard, put it in the mix, and return it to the cupboard all in one movement. When washing clothes, put the item straight from the dryer into a basket labeled for the appropriate person. The list goes on and on, but as I implemented the principle, I found that the clutter began to disappear.

All in all, I can honestly say that after I started putting away all my own things, saw to it that my own bed was the first one made, and followed through with making the children responsible for their things, our home became a different place. I would not have believed that it could make so much difference!

I am a firm believer in the saying, "Thing order precedes thought order." It is almost impossible for me to get my mind functioning smoothly if I am surrounded with clutter and unable to find anything I need.

In getting your home in order you first must decide what you *really* want. You can do anything you deem absolutely necessary—but it isn't easy. Keep in mind also that one mother's definition of order is very different than another's. "I spend *my* time on the *children*," said one messy mother with a smile. Remember as you think through the process of order in your home that you do have to set standards in your family's mind and then—the hardest part—be consistent. However, you also have to remember, as you grind those rusty wheels of better household order into action and establish a working system, that although you can do anything you really want, you can't do everything.

You can spend so much time on your home—cleaning and putting things in order—that you neglect the children. Find a system that has a happy medium, that produces a comfortable order level but also involves the principle of "selective neglect." I personally don't believe it's possible for a mother with a young family to keep everything perfect all the time. Sometimes, as the "new" saying goes, "It isn't pretty being easy."

Wonderful mothers have produced charts and awards, plans and schemes by the thousands to keep children excited about carrying out responsibilities and keeping things in order. I used to start thinking that we were doing all right, and then I would hear of a new, exciting system that absolutely astounded and inspired me. This book is not designed to detail all those elaborate plans. My goal here is to encourage you to come up with your own plan, one that you feel comfortable using with your own family. Make your plan exciting for the children and base it on a system with lots of rewards and a few punishments. Then be consistent to help them achieve excellence. Just last week, I heard of a mom whose system revolved around kids owing her fifteen minutes of cleaning time on Saturday if they didn't make their beds in the morning. The possibilities are endless.

A good friend advocates (and I agree with her) the principle of changing the system of rewards at least every three months to keep the kids excited. The end results remain the same, but the children get a fresh breath of air to try again.

We like to keep our systems fairly simple. Sometimes if things get too elaborate they become a pain instead of a help.

I would like to mention a few basics that have helped us a great deal in establishing better order in our home. After taking a good look at the frequent "disaster areas" (the little ones' rooms), we decided that the biggest culprits were: (1) dressers to hang clothes out of, (2) closets where everything accidentally dropped to the floor, and (3) beds under which to hide toys, Sunday suits with mashed potatoes squashed on them, schoolwork, empty dog-food cans, half-eaten apples, and an amazing assortment of other treasures. Our solution may sound a bit extreme, and I'm sure most of you will not be ready to run right out and try this tomorrow, but it might give you some ideas.

Because we were remodeling the kitchen and laundry room of our home anyway, we decided to do it with order and convenience for *our* family in mind. We enlarged the kitchen in two directions to create a better flow of traffic and to accommodate the hundreds of bodies in and out each week.

Then we decided to turn an unfinished area in the basement into a "nerve center." We removed the dressers from all the children's rooms except those of the two oldest girls (who did a good job of taking care of their own things) and built a "unit" in the laundry room for each of the five younger children (we had seven children at the time). Each unit consisted of four drawers: one for shirts, one for pants, one for pajamas, and one for underclothes and socks. Under the four drawers we put a bin for shoes. Above the drawers were two square shelves for treasures, school projects, and special possessions, and to the right was a tall opening for violins, tennis racquets, and baseball bats. Above that were two shelves that only I (or Richard) could reach: One for seasonal clothes (winter clothes in summer, summer clothes in winter) and the other for hand-me-downs that the child was about to grow into. The units were part of the laundry room so that the children could go there, take off dirty clothes, and put them in the appropriate bins (one for darks, one for mediums, and one for whites), and choose clean clothes or pajamas.

When I did the washing, the clothes went directly from the bins to the washer, dryer, folding table, and back into the drawers—all within six or eight steps. There were also two bars for hanging clothes and four shelves for Mom, Dad, and the two big girls, where we could pick up our things once a week and put them in our rooms.

We also took all the toys out of the bedrooms and put them in one toy area with shelves and drawers where they belonged when not in use.

With no clothes or toys or dressers in the children's rooms, things became much simpler. Each child had a bed, a nightstand with special books to read at bedtime, and pictures and decorations on the walls that made him happy.

I admit that the children still managed to cut up bits of paper in their rooms and do a good job once in a while of making a pretty fair mess, but by and large about 75 percent of the clutter was eliminated. They usually took great pride in seeing that their rooms were clean before they went to school because it wasn't an insurmountable job. Even our tiny boys (ages three and two) loved making their beds

The Unit

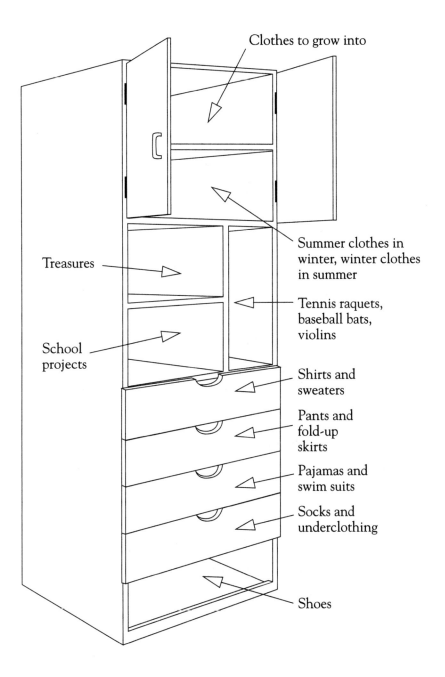

Clothes to grow into

Summer clothes in winter, winter clothes in summer

Treasures

Tennis raquets, baseball bats, violins

School projects

Shirts and sweaters

Pants and fold-up skirts

Pajamas and swim suits

Socks and underclothing

Shoes

(which consisted of throwing their continental quilts up around their pillows).

You may not be ready to remodel your home, but consider rearranging it. Put all the dressers in the laundry room and all the toys in a toy room. Don't leave the little children anything to make a mess with. Teach the little ones that their clothes can be in only one of three places: on their bodies, in their units, or in the "dirty bins." As children are old enough to take pride in their things, reward them by moving dressers and toys back into their rooms.

Another major necessity for order in the home (as much as I hate to admit it) is getting up in the morning. This has been hard for me ever since I was a child and used to get up at 6:00 A.M. and put on my mother's old beaver coat to keep me warm in the cold room where the piano was.

Some mothers of preschoolers love schedules—love getting up early and getting things done before the kids wake up. I'm sorry to report that I wasn't one of them. When our little ones were preschoolers, I enjoyed to the fullest my freedom of not having to meet everyday schedules, because I had the feeling that it wouldn't last long—and it didn't!

I basically hate schedules. I hate doing things at the same time every day, but I've learned through the school of hard knocks that for a family with lots of children it's the best way.

To this day I can't wait until the Christmas holidays and summer vacations so that we can just relax and do what we want to do.

I truly envy you who "pop out" at 5:00 A.M. and get it all together. As a mother of young children, I did my best to drag myself out at 6:00 or 6:15 at the latest to make sure the first two practicers were ready to begin on the downbeat of 6:30.

If we had breakfast and prayers at 7:30 and got our "junior higher" out the door and rooms checked by 8:00, and everybody off to school on time, I felt as if we'd really accomplished something. Maybe that sounds easy to some of you early birds, but for us night owls it's a major project! I've discovered that getting things done in order, the same way every day, helps children feel secure and orderly.

Another basic rule of thumb is never to go to bed with a dirty kitchen. (By that I mean dirty dishes and clutter.) It took me several years to figure out that it is much harder to face a sink full of dirty dishes in the morning than it is late at night—no matter *how* tired you are. I remember feeling terribly depressed because it often took me until noon to get the kitchen back in order again after a busy night. (Just in time to mess it up again with lunch.) Even if you are tripping over toys to get there, a clean kitchen is like a breath of encouraging air first thing in the morning.

When you get the kitchen mastered, take a quick run through the rest of the house to be sure things are put away at night. The benefit in the morning is immeasurable. During really busy times we find it also helps to set the breakfast table and prepare the orange juice at night. On school days we have a fairly set menu for each day so that nobody has to wonder what to fix. (Of course there are always those days when you're out of milk *and* eggs, and then a creative idea or two really helps.)

Order is the key to many things in a busy household. Even

though I still can rarely find a brush, a pen, or a pair of scissors, I can honestly say that things have gotten better over the years.

One other tidbit is the fact that order begins with you. Get yourself ready and your bed made first! Resolve that you're never going to "mush" through the kitchen in your nightgown and bare feet to meet the mailman in your bathrobe again (at least on school days)! It makes everybody feel better about having a good, productive day if you look ready to stand at the helm first thing in the morning.

Challenges

1. Analyze the order situation in your home and decide what needs to be done to improve it. Consult with the kids and then (with a few ideas to guide them) decide together on a system that is fun and rewarding for everyone.

2. Stick to it! It took us many years before we could say that things were *really* getting better (I hope you're all smarter—sooner). After you've reached a satisfactory level of order, remember that everything can't always be perfect. Don't sweat the small stuff.

3. Get up and get going. Get up before the kids, and/or train them so well that things go along smoothly even when you're in bed sick, nursing, or pregnant.

23

Expand Your Horizons

"All work and no play makes Mom a dull girl!" Although it seems impossible to do anything more than clean, cook, and care for children, it is very important to keep learning and keep growing.

Sometimes a mother feels selfish taking her precious time from the children to do something she wants to do, but I like to think about it the opposite way. We are better mothers when we have creative outlets to free our minds periodically; our growing and progressing helps our children. We can teach only what we know. The greater the variety of interests to which we can expose our children, the better educated they are. Don't leave it all up to someone else!

Of course, I'm not implying that you should go back to school full time so that you can teach your children art or economics. The time for that (for most of us) has passed for a while. But there is an abundance of things that you can do to enrich your life—even *with* a troop of small children.

Find ways to actively use the gifts you've been given. If you're an artist, start an art class among mothers for fun and enjoyment. If you love to read, create a book club that meets once a month to discuss a certain pre-assigned book. If you love cooking, create a rotating dinner group and perhaps choose food from another country once a month to share together. If you love dancing, find a neighbor or relative who can take your children for just two hours once a week, and dance away. Or take an aerobics class—nurseries are often provided.

It is always easier not to get involved in the hassle of arranging things and getting the kids ready and out the door, but the extra effort is almost always worth it!

My particular love is music. I was a string major in college, and though I was terrified to play by myself, I loved playing in groups. Many years ago, when we were first married, I found a wonderful group of "kindred spirits" while we lived in Washington, D.C., with whom I played in a string quartet. It was their love and support that changed my terror of performing into a love for it. The group consisted of another violinist, Cheryln; a cellist, Carolyn; and a violist, another Carolyn. (I always regretted that my name wasn't Marilyn.)

Richard and I moved away from these "soul sisters" for almost eight years, and then went back to Washington to find that they were all still there, ready to play. Our circumstances had changed somewhat by then, however: Among the four of us we had twenty-six children and two grandchildren.

After our first rehearsal we were so thrilled to be playing together again that we pledged ourselves to prepare a forty-five minute concert to be presented in three months, just before we moved again.

No one would believe the riotous times we had together at rehearsals. If we could have taped the practices, unedited, they would easily have been funnier than any sitcom you see on TV.

In the first place, we rehearsed with at least seven preschoolers under foot. (We learned to practice with our feet on our music stands to keep the crawling babies from tipping them over.) One

Carolyn was the president of a large women's organization and always had to dash in between meetings to get to our practices. The other Carolyn had to drive forty-five minutes one way to get to the rehearsals and would come in her teenager's car (which looked a lot like it had just been through the trash masher) in between car pools and the frantic schedules of her eight children. Cheryln had a nursing baby, and though we tried to convince her to learn to nurse and play the violin at the same time (mothers have to learn to do almost any *other* two actions simultaneously), she opted to hum her part while we played and she nursed.

Someone was always late, and there were usually two or three rounds of calls before we worked out a satisfactory "next rehearsal" time. But when we got together—did we ever have a great time! We loved making beautiful music together.

Every rehearsal was an adventure. About every eight minutes one of the roving pack of little ones needed a Band-Aid, a rescue from a bad dog, a peanut-butter sandwich, a clean diaper, or a mediator for negotiations on toys. Other than that, they danced together to the music and once even took off all their clothes and had a great romp in the little plastic swimming pool in the backyard. At the end of a movement, Carolyn often found my baby hanging on the end pin of her cello, gazing up at her.

We performed many times together during those few months at ladies' luncheons and rest homes. It was always an unbelievable hassle, but the night of our *big* recital topped them all in more ways than one.

One Carolyn had just returned from a two-week trip to Hawaii, China, and Egypt, and we had practiced ferociously the last two days. The night of the performance she called to ask if I could drive, because she had just realized that the insurance had expired on her car. I was frantically packing boxes and sweating out our move the next day. The air conditioner in our house was broken and it was 95 degrees with 95 percent humidity. I had been about to call her to tell her that there was a flat tire on our car and we had no spare. We decided on the uninsured car.

When we got there, a little later than planned, the other Carolyn and Cheryln, who had had to come from the other direction on the beltway, still had not arrived. When they did arrive (huffing and puffing and red-faced) one explained that her husband had been held up and didn't get home to take over the kids. The other said she had had a van full of cases of grapefruit that her kids were selling for a fund-raising project at the high school. Somehow the brake had released and the van had coasted across the street into the neighbor's tree, scattering grapefruit everywhere, not to mention the damage to car and tree. We all got the giggles about being so "true to the end" and then settled down to the seriousness of the task ahead.

I must admit that my eyes filled with tears during the last piece we played, "Canon in D" by Johann Pachelbel, a work that we all loved. My mind wandered back to all the wonderful times we'd had together talking and playing and enjoying in spite of the adversity. How easy it would have been for any *one* to say, "I'm too busy. Let's do that when the kids are grown." (In this case we knew it was now or never.)

Of course there are many things that we do have to give up at certain times in our child-rearing years. Only you can judge when the children are suffering rather than benefiting from a too-busy, too-strung-out mom. Do the things that you really feel will benefit you *and* the children most. If your desires require your kids to spend long hours with a baby-sitter for an extended period, you might want to wait.

Another way to expand your horizons is to form a mothers' group, a group of young mothers with whom you feel very comfortable. Start small, two or three will do, or go to five or six if there is a natural group that seems to gel. Then do something more than just go out to lunch together! I'm convinced that women are a great comfort and help to one another—even women with wonderful husbands and no major problems.

The first group I was involved in was such great fun! We were all young moms with one or two tiny children. We met together once a month and set some common goals. We all decided that our biggest problems were (1) getting up early enough in the morning and (2) reading the scriptures daily. We decided that we needed to get up to be effective (times ranged from 5:00 A.M. to 7:30) and we also decided on a certain amount of scriptures to read before we met again. We called each other periodically to "check up." We all made great progress.

Another group formed in a different location spent time talking about everything from new recipes to child discipline. Still another group concentrated more on reading something each month that was particularly pertinent to the pressures of mothering, and then discussing it.

The women in each of these groups have a special, warm place in my heart for the things that they taught me. It was wonderful to discover that other mothers were struggling with the same things I was, and often had solutions I hadn't thought of.

The group I'm involved with now has decided to have each woman read independently on a different subject each month and then report to the others on her findings. Last month we talked about "inspiring women." We hope to get into things like political figures and the lives of composers and artists. It's impossible to do all the reading that you'd like to when children are small, but it's nice to have some help and at the same time to form forever friendships.

Learn, Then Teach

Among all the hats that a mother must wear—cook, cleaner, car pooler, negotiator, washer, sorter, repair person—there is one hat that may be more important than all the others put together: the teacher's hat.

It is easy to get priorities mixed up and to spend 99 percent of your time struggling with the things that seem most pressing while neglecting the things that are most valuable and enduring.

It has been said that children never stop learning, even for a moment. But *what* they are learning is not always what we think we are teaching. We teach by example every day, and sometimes children learn things that we'd rather not have them know, such as how to manipulate people, how to get mad, or how to be continually late.

Mothers should take their jobs as teachers very seriously and not limit their teaching to the things that children happen to learn through example. Decide what you want your children to learn and then go for it! Contrary to what you might sometimes like to think, school and church do not teach your children all that they need to know. Parents are really the prime source of a child's education!

Most public schools, despite their efforts and good points, do not adequately teach communication skills (writing, reading, speaking, listening), questioning and research methods, or the arts. And one thing that they are often forbidden to teach is values. Because honesty, courage, love, kindness, and self-discipline are crucial values for a child to learn in this crazy mixed up world, Richard and I have designed audiotapes that teach these values one month at a time. They are available through our Homebase Organization. If you're interested in these at-home values programs, contact the Homebase office at 1615 Foothill Boulevard, Salt Lake City, Utah 84108.

Volumes could be written about teaching these subjects to children in your home. But we try to concentrate on only one value per month. For example, we say, "This month we're going to focus on honesty. At our family meeting next week we'll be sharing ways we were able to be honest this week." (This is as good for the parents as it is for the kids!)

In addition, we have found that when we are able to be together around the dinner table we can occasionally conduct fifteen-to-twenty-minute educational sessions for the children. On Mondays, we might start these dinner sessions with speeches. Each child stands, in turn, and speaks extemporaneously on an assigned topic for sixty seconds. On Wednesdays, we might start dinner with "the question game," in which Richard or I mention a topic and each child asks the best question he can think of on that topic. This has often led us to the family encyclopedias for some interesting research after dinner. On Fridays, the children might write short themes or poems that they can read to the family during dinner.

Another valuable teaching time during the day is when the children are just home from school. As they unwind from a hectic day, have them dance to or listen to great music instead of letting them become glued to the "know-nothing nonsense" on TV.

Much of the real joy in parenting comes from teaching children to appreciate the finer things in life through music, art, dance, and literature. Often the greatest challenge for this type of teaching is that you must first educate yourself. Few things can lift your spirits to "a higher realm" more quickly than the fine arts. Even if it takes extra time and effort for you to educate yourself, the return will be invaluable.

Let me suggest a few simple methods in each area that may spark ideas of your own.

Art. While visiting with some friends a few years ago I noticed nine small prints of famous paintings on the wall of the family room. When I inquired about them the mother stated that the family was studying art together. Every member of the family (from Mom and Dad down to the three-year-old) knew who had painted each picture and what kind of picture it was (classical, impressionistic, and so on). Their three-year-old pointed out her favorite and, when asked who painted it, answered with a smile, "Mikoangewo."

You can appreciate the world much more fully if you educate yourself and your children to see the beauty of art—including color, form, and texture.

Music. The amount of wonderful music to which you can expose your children is almost endless, but try starting with one of these well-beloved classics (easily found in most libraries): "Peter and the Wolf," by Sergei Prokofiev; "The Planets," by Gustav Holst; "Pictures at an Exhibition," by Modest Mussorgsky; "The Sorcerer's Apprentice," by Paul Dukas; or "Ride of the Valkyries," "Forest Murmurs," or "The Magic Fire Music" from *The Ring* by Richard Wagner.

Do some research (there is usually quite a lot of information on the backs of album covers) on the pieces and explain the "stories" to your children as you play them. Learn to love them together, and fine music will be a treasure throughout your lives.

When you can, expose your children to live concerts and artists. Don't try to do too much at once. (Try leaving at intermission—before your "Cub Scouts" become restless—and go for ice cream.)

Dance. There are two simple ways for children to appreciate dance: to watch it and to do it. We are always amazed at how exciting it is to watch our children dance. Put on any of the pieces of music just mentioned, or one of your own favorites, and watch their personalities pop out before your very eyes. Boys and girls, young and old alike cannot help but have an exciting experience in making their bodies move to beautiful music.

If you have an opportunity to take them to a ballet, such as *The Nutcracker* or *Swan Lake*, check or purchase beforehand a good recording of the ballet to use as "background music" for your daily activities for a couple of weeks. You'll be amazed at the difference it makes if the music is familiar.

Literature. Richard and I believe that one of the greatest series of books a child can read (on his own from about age ten) or have read to him (down to age three) is *The Chronicles of Narnia* by

C. S. Lewis. Not only are these tales well written, but the principles of life taught therein are wonderful.

Of course a list of the Newberry Award winners is an excellent guide to good reading. Every child should read *Charlotte's Web* and (every girl at least) *The Little Princess*, but don't limit yourself to those. There are many wonderful classics available that are extremely enlightening and enriching for young children to give them a head start on their formal education in literature.

One summer I read with our eleven-year-old *A Tale of Two Cities* by Charles Dickens. Although a good dictionary and a lot of explanations were necessary, it was a wonderful experience for us both.

One marvelously effective way to get children to read is to give them a choice between reading and going to sleep. While we were in England we got used to the practice of early bedtimes. Our children learned that they must observe a specific (and rather early) bedtime, but that they had a full hour before lights out *if* they wished to use it for reading.

In short, remember that the greatest gift you can give your children is a knowledge of the wonders and beauties found in the finer things of life. In imparting these things, you can expand your own horizons and feel yourself learning and growing as a mother.

Challenges

1. Discover ways to expand your horizons. Use your gifts before you lose them. Decide what would best benefit you and your children at this point in time and go after it tenaciously.

2. Form a mothers' group with inspiring friends who can help you expand your horizons.

3. Turn off the TV and *read*.

4. Learn, then teach. Concentrate on one area at a time. Do some research on each subject so that you can teach it more effectively. Bring a "higher realm" to your home by exposing your children to values and the fine arts.

24

Guard Your Most Valuable Possession— Your Body

What's wrong with me? I thought as a young mother at the end of a grueling day with the children. *Why can't I get this family going? It seems that all I do all day is give ignored instructions and try to squelch arguments. I'm just the fire extinguisher around here!*

For several weeks it seemed that every child, each half hour or so, had gone the rounds—someone would smash a finger in a door, then subsequently be shoved or banged by a sibling, then start whining that he was "*starving.*" When all seven got going at once, I felt like the old woman in the shoe about to explode her laces.

Even my husband had noticed me jumping on the children for very unimportant things and answering every request with an irritated voice and an annoyed gesture. That evening we went for a drive, just Richard and me. It took several hours of ranting and raving about how I never felt that my time was my own and how I was sick to death of squabbling, injured children, before I figured out what was wrong. I rationalized that it was the new environment. (We were vacationing for a month in Jackson Hole, Wyoming.) For several weeks I'd been obsessed with packing, cleaning, and tying up loose ends on church responsibilities. The night before the trip, eight-year-old Josh had fallen off a fence and broken his arm, so we'd spent five valuable hours of packing time at the hospital. The morning we went to catch the plane, six-year-old Saydi smashed her finger in the van door, and two days after our arrival in Jackson, five-year-old Jonah had fallen out of the loft and lay on a bed for two days afraid to move for fear it would hurt.

That must be the reason for my short temper and general irritation, I thought, as I drove over to the other side of the mountain with Richard so that he could sign up for the annual tennis tournament.

As we walked into the racquet club in Jackson, however, the real cause for my irrational behavior suddenly came into focus. I unraveled it out loud on the way home, rattling off my frustrations nonstop to my poor, unsuspecting husband: "True, things have been hectic lately, but when I saw you walk into that racquet club *again*, I realized that I was angry because it seemed that you always— above everything else—have fun! You are always off to a job, off to fish, off to play tennis, and I am up to make breakfast, up to settle arguments, up to clean the fridge, up to oversee practicing, and up to make sure children's responsibilities are fulfilled. I feel physically sloggy and mentally drained."

Try as I might to blame someone else for all that, I could only come up with one person at fault: *me!* For several weeks I had neglected to have a good "Sunday Session." I *had* sketched out a rough draft of the week with "Pack and Survive" as the vague head- ing, but had neglected to set any specific goals for myself or anyone else in the process.

Even more important than that, I felt, was the fact that I had been physically inactive for many months. I had rationalized that I was too busy to get involved in an exercise class and too tired to jog, and that surely running up and down stairs and lifting babies, boxes, and brooms was enough exercise. That frame of mind had become a bad habit.

Let me preface this next episode with the fact that I am not an athletic person. Even having been raised by the basketball star of Wyoming—best broad jumper, high jumper, mile runner (my mother)—didn't help. I abhorred baseball in the fourth grade because I was so hopelessly afraid that I was going to get hit in the face with a ball. I was always grateful when I got a bloody nose so I couldn't play. Basketball was even worse. I just couldn't get the rhythm of step, bounce, step, bounce.

For me, the thought of getting up to jog when I first became conscious in the morning seemed about as pleasant as putting a worm on a hook. Even with my acknowledged "unathleticness," however, I looked back over the last few years and realized that the times I had felt most happy, most excited about doing things with the kids, and most organized correlated with the times I had been taking yoga or aerobics classes or jogging.

Even though I knew physical fitness was important, I was putting everything else in first priority. In thinking my situation over carefully, I realized that mothers really have to put themselves first in order to get everything else running smoothly. Physical fitness is the key to many other things, no matter how painful it is in some of our cases.

The very next morning I dragged myself out of bed thinking, *Surely I can start this tomorrow; it looks so cold outside. In fact, it's actually snowing!* However, after the first hundred yards down the road with low clouds hanging in sheets around the Grand Tetons, and soft, big flecks brushing on my cheeks, and my lungs filling with clean, clear, cold air, as I listened to cattle mooing in the meadow, I wondered how I could ever have missed it. I felt my muscles perk up with unbelief—they were being used again, and it felt wonderful!

How can I fit that in? I had asked myself the night before, and had realized that it was only another rationalization. I am the master of my own fate. Most husbands would be delighted to be asked to listen to or feed children for fifteen minutes before work while you clear out your cobwebs. If husbands aren't there, older children or a co-op system with a neighbor can be organized. Every person has her own level of need. Physical fitness, whether it be jogging or some other form of aerobics, is not only nice but essential to make you the best mother and wife you can be!

I returned home that morning and accepted egg on the carpet and cat food on the couch, the baby throwing food, and a black look from a child who doesn't like eggs—all with a smile and a determination to correct with a pleasant voice and control my temper regardless of the circumstances. Although obviously not a cure-all, it had already begun to help.

Perils and Ponderings of Pregnancy

The best asset a pregnant woman can have is an understanding husband. Unfortunately, it took us several pregnancies to figure out that I very consistently said and did things during a pregnancy (especially in the first few months) that were very unusual. In addition to crying when someone won a car on *Let's Make a Deal*, I got angry at almost everything. So, in my later pregnancies, when I started raving, the light would dawn on my husband after a few brief episodes and he would call a family council.

Richard would sit me down on a chair and say to the "audience": "See this woman right here? She's your mother and she's about to be somebody else's mother! We all need to understand that when Mommy is pregnant she gets mad really easily. I know it seems like she's mad at you; but she's not. She's just mad! I'll tell you what to do when Mommy gets mad. Just put your arm around her and tell her you know she doesn't mean to be mean!" It didn't always work exactly the way Richard envisioned, but it certainly helped. At least the kids understood a little better and tried to help!

And so, when I would get on my high horse with Richard and start making crazy, wild statements, he would put his arm around me and say, "I know you don't mean that!" Even though I always violently protested that I did mean it, I usually realized within a half-hour that I really didn't.

Husbands, Beware—and Help! We Need It!

Mothers, don't expect too much of yourself during a pregnancy. Sometimes schedules have to slide for a while when you're too nauseated to get out of bed.

If you fall asleep while you're reading stories to your three-year-old and are a grump during dinner, just remember—"This, too, will pass."

Diet is much more important during the childbearing and rearing years than at any other time in life. Not only does your body depend on it during that crucial time; but the proper formation of another body is at stake.

As research has increased on how much a fetus is affected by the physical health of its mother—even before conception—we have learned that eating, sleeping, and exercise habits make a marked difference in creating healthy children. Certainly there is no more important time to be concerned about and actually working on having a healthy body.

Often irritability or inability to cope with stressful situations is a direct result of not only hormonal imbalances but also vitamin or iron deficiencies due to the lack of proper exercise. Your body can easily be called your most valuable earthly possession. When something is wrong with it, everything else seems wrong. On the other hand, when you feel great, there's nothing you can't do!

Although there are times when physical exercise is cut to a minimum because of a pregnancy or a new baby, don't rationalize your way back into the physical doldrums. Don't think you are sacrificing exercise and a good diet because you're too busy taking care of your family.

It's impossible to go into detail about exactly how much physical exercise is appropriate, especially during a pregnancy, because every body is different. Some mothers stick to tennis, aerobics, or the latest exercise video right up to the delivery day. Others may have to go to bed for nine months to save the baby. Check with your doctor and use your own good sense in knowing what is best for you.

Don't make the mistake of thinking you must eat for two during a pregnancy—and end up the size of two after your baby is delivered. Neither should you starve yourself to death so that you can have your "model's" figure back two weeks after delivery.

Again, you need to analyze your own body, your metabolism, and your needs, and then come up with a plan to maintain it at a satisfying level, so that when the pregnancy is over, you don't have to feel depressed about looking terrible and struggling to lose fifteen pounds while you're nursing a baby. An ounce of prevention *is* worth a pound of cure!

Challenges

1. Although hormone imbalances are often the culprit, remember that your irritability level often has to do with your diet and exercise. Put yourself first for the benefit of everyone else in your family and stick to a good physical fitness program and diet.

2. Don't expect too much of yourself during pregnancy, but do take fastidious care of your body. Eating right, exercising, and feeling good about you are crucial! (Don't worry about your feet; they're still there, you just can't see them for a while.)

25

Be Flexible

Now that we have gone through a long list of fairly specific things that a mother can do to cope with stress, I cannot close without stating what may seem to be the antithesis of many of the things we've just discussed: Be flexible!

An article in the *Washington Post* told of a woman who had wanted to survey families firsthand to find whether there was a common thread in well-adjusted families as well as in the unhappy ones. In order to feel that her study had some depth, she decided to actually live with each family for a period of one month. Her survey involved twenty families from all different social and economic levels. Many of her findings were vague because she found each family to be so different. But one thing that she could single out as a common characteristic of the happiest families was that they were "flexible."

The columnist didn't explain herself in great detail, but did indicate that flexibility did not mean that members of the family were not high achievers, only that when situations arose that required things to happen at a different time or place, the change occurred without a great deal of fuss.

Being flexible doesn't mean eliminating goals or plans when they aren't convenient. It simply means finding a better time to do them (or if not better, at least more convenient). It also means facing the reality that sometimes instead of doing something a few hours or days or even years later, you might have to accomplish your goal in an entirely different way.

Flexibility may mean putting away the fabric you bought to make Christmas clothes until Valentine's Day or next Christmas. Sometimes it may even mean putting a hobby or even a career you love on the top shelf until your children are older. It may mean that an intense daily schedule that really works must be relaxed because of morning sickness or the arrival of a new baby. Once in a while it means taking the kids to church with two heads unwashed and one set of unmatched socks. It may mean dropping some parsley around a molded salad that dropped out of its mold like a glob of wet plaster of Paris on the day of your special luncheon and saying to yourself, "Never mind, they'll never know what it should have looked like anyway." It may even mean giving up a wonderful vacation that you've planned on for months, because of a family illness or death.

Situations arise every day that require us to decide if we're going to be flexible. Sometimes we realize that we can fit in taking a meal to an unexpectedly sick friend on an already hectic day. Sometimes flexibility requires us to realize that someone else could truly help a friend in need better than we could, even though we'd rather do it ourselves.

One of a mother's great keys of flexibility is the use of lateral thinking—a thought process advocated by Edward de Bono, born in Malta and educated at Oxford and Cambridge Universities. He tells a story of a merchant's daughter to illustrate lateral thinking. It seems that the merchant had the misfortune of owing a large sum to a ruthless creditor. The old and ugly creditor fancied the merchant's beautiful daughter and said he would cancel the debt if he could have the girl instead.

Seeing that the daughter was horrified at the proposal, the creditor proposed that they let providence decide the matter. He picked up two pebbles from the pebble-strewn path, put them in his hat, and told the girl that if she drew the white pebble he would release the debt and leave them alone. If she drew the black pebble, however, she would have to go with him. The girl, sharp-eyed with fright, saw that he had slipped two black pebbles into his hat instead of one of each color.

She employed lateral thinking. She pulled a pebble from the hat and, without looking at it, fumbled and dropped it to the path, where it was quickly lost among the other pebbles. "Oh, how clumsy of me," she said, "but never mind, if you look into the hat you will be able to tell which pebble I chose by the color of the one that is left" (*The Use of Lateral Thinking* [Harmondworth, Middlesex, England: Penguin Books, 1971], p. 241).

Our dilemmas may be not quite as dire as the one cited here, but "catch-22" type situations face us constantly as mothers. Use your mental effort to think laterally and produce creative solutions.

Lateral thinking is a careful thought process that helps us to be flexible and to get things done in a way we wouldn't have thought of through normal direct reasoning. One simple, everyday example in my life occurred on an airplane one day. Richard had been really excited about a new paperback novel he was reading and was anxious to have me read it so that we could talk about it. As I rummaged through my bag to find it while the stewardess began her "how-to-fasten-your-seat belt" procedure he said, "Where's my book? I'm at an exciting part."

"Hey, I thought this was my chance to catch up with you," I pleaded. He looked at my face as I handed him the book, thought silently for about fifteen seconds, then with a smile he gallantly tore the book in half and handed me the first half. Although it took the man across the aisle a few minutes to recover, I smiled too and wished I had thought of it first.

Challenges

1. Use lateral thinking to take a different, easier "route" to the desired end, especially when you think you've got more to do than you can handle.

2. Throw out the routine once in a while and do something crazy. Go to a midnight movie with your husband even though there's school tomorrow. Take the kids to get ice cream in their pajamas. Let your children know that you like to be crazy, too. Sleep out with them on the lawn once in a while. Drop everything and go on a spur-of-the-moment vacation for a couple of days— even if it's hard to rearrange and leave responsibilities and pack everybody up.

Everybody needs a break once in a while. Sleep in on Saturday morning even though you've got "thousands" of things to do. Serve hot dogs for Sunday dinner. Be flexible!

26

Remind Yourself How Much Fun You're Having

One beautiful autumn morning I was working on a book in my car, which was parked at a rest area on a narrow canyon road ablaze with the golds, reds, and yellows of fall. I looked up and noticed that most of the traffic going by was made up of stunning antique autos from the era of the early 1900s—all with numbers on the back, obviously ready for some sort of car rally somewhere up the road.

Being a lover of old cars, I found myself looking up to smile and admire every time one passed by. As the procession went on, I couldn't help but notice that the people in the cars were mostly old people—ladies with gray hair pulled back in buns and scarves, men in top hats, with red handkerchiefs tied around their necks. Many were in open-air cars with flawless paint jobs; some were in rumble seats and most were sitting forward in their seats, obviously drinking in the joy of the moment: the breathtaking sights and sounds and smells of autumn. All were smiling. Many honked horns and waved at anything and everything in sight (mostly leaves and rocks). They were having the time of their lives!

How wonderful it would be, I thought, *to enjoy every day like that!* My mind quickly reverted back to a conversation I'd had with Richard just the night before.

I was depressed. The kitchen had been being remodeled for about two-and-a-half months, but the metal trim had never been installed in the doorway so the linoleum was getting torn. The wallpaper had been sitting in the basement for two weeks waiting for somebody to put it up. (Having come to the end of our remodeling budget I had decided it had to be me.)

The kids were all adjusting to a new year at school. Our shy junior-high student was miserable trying to cope with being the worst player on the soccer team. Another child needed to be told to unload the dishwasher (or do anything else, for that matter) at least eight times before it got done. Our kindergartner whined from 11:30 when he got home from school until bedtime. The three-year-old had just hit the "terrible twos" a year late. Our fifth grader had banged her head on a brick wall in a P. E. class and had complained of headaches for days. Our second grader begged nonstop for friends to come over, and the baby's latest hobby was consistently messing his diaper while he was in bed and then taking the diaper off and spreading a thin coat all over the sheets, the walls, and his body. (No amount of pleading, coaxing, explaining, or spanking could change his mind.)

That, along with trying to squeeze in haircuts, birthday parties, school activities, tulip planting, children's lessons, and church meetings made me feel absolutely depressed!

"Now, wait a minute!" Richard said with a smile, in his usual down-to-earth-I've-got-a-solution-for-this-problem way. "Step back and look at yourself for a minute. You have the new kitchen you've always wanted, seven terrific kids, and a *wonderful* husband. Don't live in the past or the future. Enjoy the present—even if it's hard."

He was absolutely right. For everything that was wrong or inconvenient, I could, if I tried, think of several things that were wonderful. It's easy to live for the future: "Won't it be lovely when the baby can walk and I don't have to carry him everywhere," or for the past: "Wasn't it lovely when the baby just sat in one place and couldn't pull everything out of the cupboards or get lost!"

No matter what is happening in your life, there is a great deal of joy to be experienced at that moment—if you only take the time to realize it. Of course, gratitude is one of the keys to feeling joy and enjoying each day—gratitude for good health, a warm home, a husband who cares, parents who still keep helping, and children who have their own opinions.

Don't misunderstand me. I'm not saying that every moment should be filled with joy; that is simply not possible. I realized this one Christmas when I was coping with the fact that preparing for Christmas was not the "every-day-more-exciting-and-wonderful" scenario I had envisioned from the storybooks. This is especially true when the two-year-old opens all the presents on December twenty-first and a couple of kids get diarrhea or croup to add to the holiday cheer. The real joy of Christmas comes in a few special moments when, for example, you watch your six little dears really put their hearts into singing, "O Come All Ye Faithful" on somebody else's doorstep, or you see the joy in Jonah's face as he hands Talmadge the gift he has bought with his own hard-earned money. These moments make all the quarrels, wasted Scotch tape, food dribbled down the cupboard doors, and endless hours of shopping and preparing fade into one big lump of "necessary hazards," and those ten or twelve really special sets of moments stand out like beacons!

Every week has those special moments, if you just watch for them. It is too easy to dwell on the negative and not even see the positive, let alone comment on it. How often do you go into a playroom and say, "I love the way you two are playing nicely together," as opposed to the number of times you become angry over quarrels or misbehavior and yell, "Okay, you guys, who did this?"

Make a conscious effort to be positive. Tell your children the things you appreciate and like about them. They often don't even realize those things! Compliment them on putting toys away or getting homework done without being told, instead of just expecting it or nagging at them when they don't.

A friend gave me a great idea: "I go into the children's rooms every night that I'm home to tuck them in," she began. "I make a conscious effort when I walk into the room to turn off all the problems and 'negatives' of the day and turn my mind to something that that child has done during the day that was helpful or admirable. Sometimes it's really hard, but even if the deed is only tiny, I tell him about it." Sincere appreciation and compliments go a long way. They "calm the savage beast" and inspire the child to do something even better tomorrow.

Little things—kindness, sharing, obedience—frequently slip past without being mentioned. When we let this happen, we lose a golden opportunity to let our children know that we think they're terrific, in spite of any minor flaws they may possess.

Love the Present

Amidst whines and wails of a hard afternoon, and after five days of being without Richard, I looked up to see him pull in the driveway and start to unload presents from the back of his car.

It seemed that those five days of being mother *and* father had been full of hard decisions, such as not letting Saydi stay overnight with a friend because the last time she had stayed up all night she had been unbearable for three days afterward. Heartbroken, she had bawled like a sick cow and in her own feisty way was heard to say under her breath as she stomped off to her room to get over it, "I never knew you could be so mean!"

I had spent that afternoon "cracking the whip" to see that responsibilities, practicing, and homework were done. A special urgency hung in the air as we all anticipated making everything look nice for Daddy.

As I watched him walk in, laden with little gifts and grinning ear to ear, my first thought was how nice it was to have him back. My second thought, however, was: "Well, here comes Santa Claus! I do all the hard stuff and he comes home and has a party!"

We can get hung up on that attitude if we're not careful: He gets to walk away from the mess every day to a nice, orderly office, and I run from one disaster to the next.

On another occasion, a cold January morning, I was feeling particularly sorry for myself. Richard had been gone for a week. He was preparing the way for our move back to our Washington, D.C., residence, to which we were returning because he had accepted the chairmanship of the White House Conference for Parents and Children. It was inauguration time, and every night he called on the phone with a glowing report of the spectacular fireworks at the Lincoln Memorial, or his meeting with the Secretary of HEW, or the wonderful time he'd had at the inaugural balls (don't worry, nobody dances, they only stand shoulder to shoulder and look at each other's party clothes).

On the afternoon of the big parade, I sat excitedly on top of the packing boxes with my nose pressed to the TV. I was sure that I would see him as the Utah delegation approached the presidential stand. Just as the announcer heralded their coming, the phone rang and I missed the whole thing. Tired and bitter, I distinctly remember thinking, "He gets to have all the fun."

Early that evening, as I had promised, the children piled in the car and, in spite of lightly falling snow, we began to hand-deliver birthday party invitations for our two children whose birthdays were within a few days of each other. They insisted that they wanted to give the invitations to their friends personally, and that just receiving them in the mail wasn't nearly as much fun, especially when they all lived in the neighborhood. Eighteen invitations were stuffed in their hot little hands, and after the first two to three I thought to myself, *You must be crazy! It's a cold, miserable winter night and you're running up and down these hills like an ant who's lost his way.*

The children always went to the door in different combinations of two, according to whose friend it was and who hadn't recently had a turn. After four or five doors I noticed something very interesting. When the duo turned from the door after placing an invitation in the hands of a friend or mother or sister, their faces were literally aglow with pleasure! They had made someone happy, and the joy shone in their faces.

After a few more doors I forgot all my woes and watched for their joyful expressions. The grins never failed. I was so sorry that

Richard was not there to see it. As that thought passed through my mind, I realized that I was really the one who was having fun! I was watching happiness ooze from our children because they were making their friends happy. What could be better? When Richard got home he agreed. He told the children how much he had missed them and how much he preferred their company to the president's!

We mothers do have fun watching these little ones learn and grow. Sometimes we're so close that we can't see it, so we have to step back a little and focus—and remind ourselves about how much fun we're having!

Richard once tried an experiment on a large audience he was speaking to. He asked all those with eight or more children to stand. There were seven couples who rose. One had sixteen (a combination of yours, mine, and ours), one fourteen, one eleven, and so on. He asked each couple to describe one moment that they remembered most vividly when they had felt a great amount of joy as a family.

All of the answers were extremely interesting and insightful, but the one that I was most impressed by was given by a beautiful silver-haired woman who stood by herself. "I don't know exactly what to say," she said. "We raised eight sons and every day was pure joy! I guess the moment that stands out most clearly may sound a little strange. It occurred while I was standing with all eight sons around the casket of my husband on the day of his funeral. I looked at those good, strong, loving sons and felt more joy than I had ever known. I realized that *we had made it,* my husband and I. We had raised eight wonderful people who were actively contributing to the betterment of their own families, their church, and their community."

I was touched by her feelings, but as much as I appreciated what she was saying, I was stunned by her first statement, "*Every day was pure joy.*" I couldn't say that every one of my days had been sheer joy by any means, and we didn't even have all boys! What was I doing wrong?

As she continued to talk, it dawned on me. *She had forgotten!* There had to have been hard days: trials, sickness, broken arms, lost merit badges, forgotten homework, and even a little rebellion, but when it was all over and she had done her best—and been successful—she had forgotten the bad times and remembered only the joy. I think there is a lesson in that for all of us. As we get older we tend to forget the hard times and replace them with the good—something wonderful to look forward to! The nice part about it is that the kids forget too. All the temper tantrums and unfair punishments will melt into memories of a happy childhood.

Time Marches On

When our oldest child turned twelve, I underwent a definite mothering crisis. The children were growing up! *Someday these children will walk out the door on their own. They will "fly the coop." Someday I won't be changing diapers anymore, except for the grandchildren's,* I thought.

Although it seems impossible, someday you'll be able to walk across the kitchen floor in slippers without picking up a quarter cup of crumbs, water, dried peas, and smashed apple on your spongy soles. Someday you'll be able to find all the brushes and pens and scissors you want, and you'll be able to walk into the kitchen without saying, "Shut the fridge door!" An end will come to the days of standing over the plumber, wringing your hands, and saying, "I can't imagine what the baby's thrown in there this time!"

Before you can believe it has happened, the children will be grown and gone. There is a different kind of joy in being grandparents, but it's not the same.

You might have occasional joy rides like the grandpas and grandmas in their old cars, but you must remember that most of them returned home that afternoon to empty houses and only the memory of how well they did as parents while they were "in the fire."

Love every moment and try to visualize each day as an exciting adventure—because tomorrow, it will be gone!

Challenges

1. Make a list of your blessings and program your mind to arise each morning with a sense of adventure rather than of doom.

2. Decide on a certain time and/or place each day to express your sincere appreciation and love to your husband and children. Try it for just one week and see if it doesn't shock your family into more loving and thoughtful patterns.

3. Look for those special little incidents during the week that remind you that *you* are the one who is really having all the fun! Record those special moments in your journal. Some of them might be classified as "disasters" to begin with, but remember the formula: "Crisis plus time equals humor."

27

Change!

After leading a parenting workshop one evening, Richard and I were approached by a young mother. "Do you ever get discouraged?" she blurted out to me. Her eyes were so full of water that one blink made the tears spill over, try as she did to keep them in. Embarrassed, she tried to flip them away, but they just kept spilling out.

I put my arm around her and remembered having felt that way so many times. "How many children do you have, and how old is your littlest one?" I asked.

"I have six children," she said as she swallowed hard. "The oldest one is seven and the baby is three months." I smiled knowingly and said, "Don't worry, things will get better. The answer to your question is unequivocally yes. Nothing can make you feel more humble and helpless than a pack of little kids." (Even one little one can do a pretty good job!)

We commiserated for a few minutes. I shed a tear or two myself, and she went away smiling, but still sniffling.

I thought about her occasionally during the next few months and even used her example in talking to other mothers to assure them that we all get discouraged. Then, a few months later, after another seminar, I looked up and there she was again. "Remember me?" she asked with a big smile. "I'm the one who was gushing with tears the last time I saw you!"

I felt a real love for her as we began talking again. During the course of the conversation she said: "You know, sometimes I say to myself, 'Why am I doing this to myself? I chose to have these children, but they're destroying my freedom! I never get to do anything I want to do. My time is totally occupied with feeding and clothing, changing and cajoling, trying to get kids to practice and put their things away, quit fighting and be kind to one another. Then," she went on, "I realized something very interesting: I am the one who is benefiting from it all. In order to survive, I have to train my mind to do things I know I should. I can feel myself becoming a little more patient and understanding. I learn how to cope with my anger and I begin to feel the true love of Christ as I watch these children learn to love each other.

"Now that my oldest has turned eight and has really started to help in a meaningful way, I can see the light at the end of the tunnel. Even though it is very difficult, I'm beginning to see that the Lord answered my prayers in giving me these children so that *I* could grow and learn and refine myself." The place where we can improve and refine ourselves most drastically—if we accept the challenge—is at home.

Overcoming Weaknesses

Progress means change. The times I grow the most are those times when I am required to change something I don't like about myself.

I heard a Sunday School lesson a few years ago that impressed me a great deal. The teacher pointed out that we often think of repentance as a long, drawn-out process that includes five steps and a lot of time. When the Savior of mankind asked us to repent, I don't think he meant it to apply only to the murderers and adulterers. He meant it to apply to us: everyday mothers with problems to work out.

In my opinion, Jesus' most adamant request, next to loving God and our fellowmen, was to *repent*. Repentance involves change. Children provide us with many great blessings. One is the absolute need to change in order to survive. A wise man once said, "If you want to be a better parent, change yourself before you try to change your children."

One of life's greatest dangers is the statement, "I know I shouldn't be that way, but I can't help it. I'd like to be different, but I just can't. That's just the way I am. I can't change."

In order to really progress in life, I believe that we are given weaknesses so that we can figure out how to turn them into strengths. In addition, weaknesses teach us how to be humble! And when we are humble (knowing that we can't do anything without the Lord's help, but also knowing that we can do everything with that help) and we have the faith that the Lord *will* help us, then weaknesses truly become our greatest strengths!

If you apply that concept, then you cannot say things like: "I'm not a good mother because I'm just not patient. My mother was very impatient and I inherited that trait. I often just can't cope with things when my children are naughty. I fly off the handle and do and say things that I regret when it's all over. That's just the way I am."

It is very comforting to know that I have a set of weaknesses to work with, and that if I really believe that I can change those weaknesses, they can actually become my strengths.

A young mother tells the story of looking down one morning just in time to see her one-year-old chomping down the last of a bottle of multivitamins with iron. Her story goes like this:

"I just laid him down, poured Ipecac syrup down him to make it come back up, put him in the bathtub with a couple of washable toys, and read a story to him while I sat on the toilet waiting for him to throw up. After three 'upchucks' I counted twenty vitamins still intact, and there was so much bright pink that I knew lots had dissolved. I thanked God for Ipecac and his help to keep me calm, and loaded my three preschoolers in the van to run an errand. As I whizzed along the freeway I heard the baby saying, 'bah-bah,' and I looked in the rearview mirror to see him pointing out the back window with a sock in one hand and a shoe in the other. The other sock and shoe were gone, and I realized that he'd been throwing everything he could find (which was a lot) out the back window.

"Once again I mustered up my calmness, pulled the van over to the side of the road, went back and retrieved a sandal that had miraculously lodged in the spare tire on the outside, and squinted my eyes to look for a bottle or shoe or any other household items on the road. Seeing none, and realizing that there was no going back and no malice intended, I got back in the van and giggled all the way to the store.

"Five years ago I would have died over that morning, but I realized on that particular occasion that after many years of working hard to remain calm even in disastrous situations, my weakness was becoming my strength. I was able to handle it with surprising ease. The Lord is really helping me! I have really changed."

One of the most glorious things about being a mother is the potential for personal growth. You don't have to go on not liking things about yourself. You can set a goal and work on a plan to grow and progress and work out the kinks in your personality. You can have all the traits necessary to develop the greatest quality of all: charity.

This quality is even more important than faith and hope, the scriptures tell us. Here is the definition: "Charity suffereth long, and is kind; charity envieth not; charity vaunteth not itself, is not puffed up, doth not behave itself unseemly, seeketh not her own, is not easily provoked, thinketh no evil; rejoiceth not in iniquity, but rejoiceth in the truth; beareth all things, believeth all things, hopeth all things, endureth all things" (1 Corinthians 13:4–7).

I challenge anyone to find a better definition of a good mother.

Charity really is attainable if you work on perfecting little things—or big things—one step at a time. Decide weekly or monthly what you'd like to change, and work on it. We can all be like Benjamin Franklin, who worked each month on one thing about himself that he wanted to improve. If you do the same, soon that good habit will become part of you, and you can begin to work on the next while keeping the last on retainer.

You can change! You can become the person you were created to be—and that exhilarating feeling of "becoming" is unparalleled to any other earthly experience. The harder it is, the more rewarding the success.

The Last Great Challenge

1. Analyze the things that you know you should change about yourself. (If you have trouble coming up with something, ask your children.) Make a list. Keep it short. Even *one* thing will be plenty for now.

2. Use all your understanding and capability to come up with a workable plan, and start to change. Use the principles of analyzing your situation, deciding in advance, holding Sunday Sessions, and making a commitment to someone else. With the help of a strong commitment, a real desire, and a faith in a God who wants you to succeed, you can do it.

You can become the mother you want to be. You can manage stress, learn to set priorities, and to put your life in order. You can spend precious quality time with each child and your husband and expand your own horizons. You can do it and become, in the truest sense, "a joyful mother of children."

Epilogue
The Harry Potter Magic of Mothering

We all love magic. When all is said and done, what we really want in our lives is magic. Many have read the tales of Harry Potter (J. K. Rowling, Books 1–3, New York: A. A. Levine Books, 1998–1999) and have loved taking the escape into a dazzling world of magic wands and Invisibility Cloaks and enchanted broomsticks. There are days when the thought of escaping into a different world if we could just find platform 9¾ is captivating.

I want to go to the magic wand store and find the *perfect* wand for me. I need one that would do the washing, drying, ironing, folding, and sock-sorting in a twinkle. One that would also do dishes and sweep the floor and suck up the dust bunnies would be good. With a grand wave and the flick of my wrist, I could command everything out of place, in its place. I'd like to watch everything find its place while the music of "The Sorcerer's Apprentice" from *Fantasia* plays in the background. Lots of beautiful colors whirling around me while they go would be nice, too.

I also yearn for one of those Invisibility Cloaks so that I could sit in the backseat on my sixteen-year-old's next date and smile, unseen. I could use it to walk around the halls of the high school with him without being an embarrassment and watch him talk and laugh with his friends. I could see somebody that looked forlorn and lonely that he might miss and tell him to befriend him or her the next day. I long to sit in my Invisibility Cloak by our thirteen-year-old during the chatter at lunch at the junior high. I could be a better teacher of how to turn the conversation from "who is weird" to "who is cool." I want to go to history and English with her and stand with her in the morning while she waits at her red locker for school to start while the popular kids giggle a few feet away in a clump. I think I could empathize instead of sermonize on the days when she thinks that her life is a miserable disaster.

I also want one of those Nimbus 2000s. That's the magic, state-of-the-art broom that seems to have a second sense about where to go to be at the right place at the right time with phenomenal speed and accuracy. I could almost instantly be at the curb where the carpool kids that I forgot about were waiting, instead of sweating it out wondering how many have called their mothers by the time I arrive. I could swoosh over traffic jams when I'm late to get a kid to the dentist and swish past the sluggish cars in the drop-off lane at school. I could fly in, out, and around my kids as they water ski in the summer, showing them a few tricks that old Mom has up her sleeve. They might even crash in awe! Yes, a little magic in an otherwise sometimes quite dreary world would be just the ticket. . . .

But wait! Recently I got a letter from our firstborn child, Saren, that was *indeed* magic. One month ago she had experienced one of life's most amazing experiences. At twenty-nine, she had brought *her* firstborn into the world. Although she and her wonderful husband had prayed along with us for the safe arrival of this new little cherub, she had just spent twenty-nine years coming and going as she pleased, filling her days with the busyness of school, then of work, then of school again. The past year she had poured her energies into life with a new job, a new husband, a move from the East to the West Coast, and a new house that needed extensive work. All the while she came and went as she needed, planned and executed her day pretty much how she wanted it to go. Having a fair idea of how different her days with a new baby would now be, I considered her letter nothing less than "the magic of mothering" personified.

One paragraph went like this: "One month ago, every time I had a little ache or pain, Jared would eagerly ask, 'Is the baby coming?' and I would go to bed every night wondering whether this might be 'the night.' It seems so unreal sometimes that all the waiting and wondering is really over and we're really parents. Our lives and the way we see each other and the world around us have changed forever—in such a good and right way. Sometimes this whole parenting thing is a little hard—like when Ashton goes through his really fussy, inconsolable period every evening for about a half hour, or when I really want to have breakfast and take a shower so we can get going on the day and he just has to be held, or when he insists on being fed even though he just ate an hour ago so I drop everything to feed him and then he won't really eat anything after all, or when he wakes up wailing at 3 A.M. and my body's SO tired I just don't know if I can really get up and feed him. But being parents is the most fulfilling and beautiful thing either of us can imagine. And we offer up prayers of gratitude every day that we were blessed with such a good baby who has brought such a wonderful spirit into our home. I look at this beautiful little baby sometimes and get a welling up of joy inside—a definite 'secret smiling of the heart.' We love stroking his soft, soft skin and kissing his sweet head with its silky blond hair. I love rocking him to sleep and seeing his angelic little sleeping face and feeling the weight of him in my arms. We love laughing at all the hilarious facial expressions he does and the funny little noises he makes. We love seeing his progress each day as he learns to focus on our faces and on objects around him. We love how he opens his big blue eyes wide and puckers up his tiny lips and looks all around in such a confused and interested manner. We love looking at his perfect tiny fingers and toes. We find ourselves talking and thinking about the little guy almost constantly. When he sleeps for several hours during the day, I find that I start to miss him, and it's so fun to pick him up and hold him again after his nap is done. So bottom line—being a mother is hard but it's so incredibly good that the hard stuff doesn't really matter much at all."

Magic! Another part that I love in the story of Harry Potter and his magical world is that he is just a poor, nerdy, mistreated little boy who has a magic secret inside—in reality he is a magnificent wizard, full of wisdom and strength and honor. Although he had had glimpses of his magic powers, he didn't really realize who he was until he was tested. Most mothers are the same way. We sort of think we have the ability to be extraordinary mothers, but what trials we have to go through to find out! There are days when we think we would never have started out on this quest, had we known about the dragons spewing fire that we would have to face. Yet the boggy swamps and seven-headed serpents have taught us creativity and ingenuity as we have maneuvered our way around them.

Personality traits have surfaced that we never would have known we had, were it not for the magical test of motherhood.

If you had told me that this awkward, outcast little seventh-grader, whose room looked as though a hurricane had been through the premises recently, could become a pretty decent mother of nine who became almost obsessed with keeping things in order, I would have declared it nothing less than magic! I would have loved to look through a crystal ball when I was an impatient young mother, tearing out my hair daily as two-year-olds made mud pies with the last of the eggs and oil, three-year-olds played "singing in the rain" with fifty pounds of popcorn in the storage room, and four-year-olds broke a quart jar of honey in the van. How fun it would have been to see the grandmother of the future, having learned some patience and perspective, smiling while watching the next generation's two-year-old "walking tornados" with glee and knowing the bigger the mess, the better the memories.

Magic happens! We *can* feel the magic of a piece of music that stirs our souls and helps us think of new ideas; we can witness a Cirque de Solei that celebrates creativity, a piece of art that moves us and makes us think thoughts beyond our normal realm of under-standing, a Broadway play that sweeps us into the magic of a differ-ent place. Poetry lifts, literature heightens our awareness, a turning point in a relationship enlightens, forgiveness releases a burden. Discovering new insights, such as learning that "less is more" and realizing that there *is* simplicity on the other side of complexity, is magic. Saydi, our dreamer-daughter who thinks she's having the most fun she's ever had teaching hard-core high school dropouts in Manhattan, describes those magical moments by saying, "There were crystals in the air." We all know exactly what she means, because we've all experienced those "crystals."

Of course there are also those lead balloons of guilt and the hard part of realizing that sometimes, the worst happens. Often you have to wade through the fire swamp to find that the best emerges from the worst. Much of the magic of mothering comes as you realize that you are learning life's simplest and most important lessons at the feet of its greatest teachers: children.

One of the hardest times in my mothering career came when our two youngest children were five and two. It was the last year when all nine children lived at home, and every day was a struggle. Problems ranged from consoling our oldest because she hadn't "been asked" to the prom to dealing with five kids in braces. On "orthodontist day," one child would inevitably forget to come out of the school at the appointed time. Another would forget his headgear. Another would be mortified to tell the doctor that he had inadvertently dropped his retainer in the garbage at McDonald's. (Although not nearly as mortified as his mother, who had to pay for a new one.) And yet another would accidentally, on purpose, leave his time chart at home because he hadn't been wearing his headgear.

On the morning of one of "those days," I took Eli, five, and Charity, two, with me to an aerobics class. In order to appreciate this story, you need to know that Charity was born after three glorious years of Eli being billed as the most spectacular baby in the world! (The longest any of our children had had the limelight before the next baby arrived). Eli had decided to make her pay for taking over his spot as the spectacular baby of the family by teasing her mercilessly. Smart little kid that he was, he had developed amazing ways to continually keep her irritated. In the process, she had developed a remarkably piercing scream, which inevitably drew immediate attention and the desired effect: a sharp reprimand to Eli from a parent or sibling. When I arrived at aerobics to find that there was no nursery, I heaved a sigh, stationed them at a place not too far, but not too close, where Eli teased and Charity screamed to my great embarrassment for the entire hour. I prayed that no one in the room knew that I had written a book called *Teaching Children Joy*.

After class I was late for the orthodontic run and I hurried out to the icy parking lot, subconsciously thinking that maybe if I got far enough ahead of Eli and Charity, no one would know that they were mine. As I approached the old van, I turned with my arms full of mats and paraphernalia, when what to my wondering eyes should appear, but Eli, with one arm firmly wrapped around Charity's shoulder and the other firmly holding her chubby little hand in his, carefully negotiating her across that icy parking lot. As it had snowed the night before, my first thought was, "He's going to find a snowbank and throw her in it before he gets to me." But not so. He just kept coming. Carefully and tenderly, he guided her to where I was standing in amazement. Finally he stopped directly in front of me. Time stood still as he stood there with one arm firmly around Charity's shoulder and his hand in hers. He gazed up at me with his wide, mischievous toothless grin and said, with a little twinkle, "Don't you wish you had a camera?"

As though a magic wand had whirled my thoughts into place, and set my priorities straight, I realized in an instant with a delighted giggle and an enormous smile that there stood before me two precious treasures. In fact at that moment, my whole life seemed like a treasure. Hassles disappeared. Life had order. There were crystals in the air. Magic!

In the End

This summer, I will have been a mother for thirty years. As I have looked back and put things in perspective, I have continued to learn that the things I thought were important when I began are not. The things I didn't even consider important are everything.

Amusingly, my first concerns when I was pregnant with our first child, other than the obvious ones about the baby's health, were about whether we would have enough money to buy our baby cute clothes. In addition, I worried about motivating the kids to be good students so they could go to the best schools. I felt that it was imperative to teach them methods to win the desires of their hearts. Though we were able to work out some of those things with varying degrees of success, all of those concerns have turned out to be mostly irrelevant. In the end, I believe the only thing truly important in rearing children is to teach them how to love—which in actuality is not something they can learn as much as it is something they can feel.

Last week Eli ran for student body president at his high school. Two years earlier, his brother Noah had run and won, and Eli was determined to do the same. There were things he wanted to do for his school, injustices that he wanted to set right, creative new ideas that he wanted to incorporate. As fate would have it, his adorable running mate for vice president was named Heidi. Richard immediately recognized that Eli and Heidi's first initials were exactly the same as the initials of the high school, East High, and so we all embarked on an "E. H. for E. H." campaign.

I must admit that as soon as I hear a child say, "I'm running for . . ." my stomach starts to churn. I can't sleep for weeks. Running for elections means that someone has to win—and someone has to lose. We've had our share of both. Winning is always more fun; yet it is also painful as you watch a friend lose. I lie awake nights the whole week worrying about the consequences of losing and the responsibilities of winning.

Actually, no one sleeps during election week. There are clever, thirty-second video clips to prepare in order to get through the two-day primary (high school elections are so much more sensible than national elections). There are pizzazzy banners to make and posters to create that cleverly articulate the campaign slogan. For Eli, there were hours of lying awake, trying to think of more ways to get votes. He was at school every morning much earlier than usual to put up banners and meet new people and ask for their votes.

On election day, the two finalists for student body president and vice president each present a two-minute skit in the auditorium that personifies their enthusiasm for leading the school. Eli and Heidi's skit involved Harley Davidson sounds and leather costumes, music from U2, and a fog machine, as well as the lowering of a huge, plywood E and H from the rafters. It was perfect!

That night, during the election stomp, all the candidates gathered in a dark room, lit only by candles, to hear the winners announced. I guess the darkness hid the smiles of those who won and the tears of those who lost. Eli lost. Hopes were smashed.

Dreams evaporated. Yet, as I watched his brave face as he was announced as the new business manager for East High (the consolation prize), and his dynamic, capable friend was named the new student body president, my mind was transported back to the events of the election week. I realized that truly, Eli had won. Although he hadn't won what he had intended to win, he had won something much more valuable. The new friends he met were important. And he had learned about perseverance, persistence, patience, perpetual problems, and poise under pressure. But even those things were not as important as the real prize.

Eli may not realize it for a while, but the most important thing that he experienced last week was the love of his friends and his family. Noah, a college freshman, had wanted Eli to win more than he had wanted to win himself when he had run. Eli tolerated the advice that Richard and I had to give, but simply couldn't wait for Noah (a much safer advisor when it came to high school kids) to get home so the real fun could begin. Noah came home from college and helped him orchestrate the music, the sound effects, and the costumes for his skit. Like a mother hen, he coached Eli on exactly what he thought would be most effective.

During the days after the election, I rewound and reviewed the events of election week. My mind pictured Richard, affectionately called Dadley by the kids, gluing photocopied pictures of every student in the high school's yearbook on Eli's banner until 1:30 A.M. In addition, he bought E and H rubber stamps, made E's and H's for posters far into the night, and was there helping Eli load things into the car early in the morning. Charity, casting thirteen years of rivalry aside, was there stamping E's and H's on posters and putting her arm around Eli, just as he had put his arm around her in their childhood.

I thought of Saydi, who had called Eli several times during the week and waited up until 3 A.M. New York City time to finally hear the news of his defeat. She was right there to give him great advice about losing (she had also lost a student body election that had almost broken her heart at the time and didn't matter one whit now).

I remembered Noah at the stomp after the announcement; his arm draped around his little brother, both with tears sparkling in their eyes and smiles on their faces. That next day, e-mails and phone calls flew through the air from all other siblings. Saren called to invite Eli to her house in California to get away and regroup and see the bigger world. Girlfriends showed up with cookies and sweet notes. Two guy friends showed up at 1:30 A.M. on the night of the election to sympathize. They stayed up all night and drowned their sorrows in their favorite video, *Dumb and Dumber*. After the sting, Eli made a miraculous recovery.

It makes me smile when I think back to my "baby" concerns about what children would wear and how I could help them win. Just as I could not have known that the most intensely difficult part of mothering is seeing a child in pain, I would never have thought that one of the greatest joys of mothering comes from seeing my children love each other. When sibling rivalry is set aside, the fierce pure love children have for their siblings is something more splendid than I ever could have imagined in my wildest dreams. In the end, winning is not important. Love is. Which is what mothering is all about.

Index